completed
1 – Mon. 6-14-76 at 10:30 P.M.

D1048599

Understandings of Man

Understandings of Man

by
PERRY LeFEVRE

THE WESTMINSTER PRESS
Philadelphia

LIBRARY OF CONGRESS CATALOG CARD NO. 66–10432

Published by The Westminster Press ®
Philadelphia, Pennsylvania

PRINTED IN THE UNITED STATES OF AMERICA

Acknowledgments

Acknowledgment is made to the following for permission to reprint their copyrighted materials:

Harcourt, Brace and World, Inc., for the poem "Confession Overheard in a Subway" in *Afternoon of a Pawnbroker and Other Poems,* by Kenneth Fearing, copyright 1943 by Kenneth Fearing.

Harper & Row, Publishers, Inc., for quotations from *New Bottles for New Wine,* by Julian Huxley, copyright 1957 by Harper & Row, Publishers, Inc.; *The Phenomenon of Man,* by Pierre Teilhard de Chardin, with an introduction by Julian Huxley, copyright 1959 by Harper & Row, Publishers, Inc.; *The Future of Man,* by Pierre Teilhard de Chardin, copyright 1964 by Harper & Row, Publishers, Inc.; *The Divine Milieu,* by Pierre Teilhard de Chardin, copyright 1960 by Harper & Row, Publishers, Inc.

New Directions for a quotation from "Handle with Care" in *The Crack-Up,* by F. Scott Fitzgerald, ed. by Edmund Wilson, copyright 1936 by Esquire, Inc., and 1945 by New Directions.

Random House, Inc., for the text of a cartoon reprinted from *Hold Me!* by Jules Feiffer, © copyright 1960, 1961, 1962, by Jules Feiffer.

United Feature Syndicate, Inc., for the text of a cartoon from *Peanuts,* © 1963 by United Feature Syndicate, Inc.

C. A. Watts & Co., Ltd., Frederick Ungar Publishing Co., Inc., and T. B. Bottomore for quotations from *The Economic and Philosophical Manuscripts,* by Karl Marx, the translation of which by T. B. Bottomore appeared in the U.S.A. in *Marx's Concept of Man,* by Erich Fromm.

Contents

Preface

THIS small book is addressed to the intelligent layman, to the college student, and to beginners in the field of theology. For many today the first serious theological questions that are asked have to do with the meaning of human existence. It is man's own nature and destiny that have become problematic. The following pages are designed to make their readers think for themselves about this problem. Except for the ninth chapter, where I have presented my own views, I have tried to remain neutral. Insofar as possible I have presented the views of others as fairly as I could in summary form. In many instances I have tried to use a given author's own words for the sake of true representation. In some cases, like that of Teilhard de Chardin, some terminology may seem strange, for Teilhard coined his own words at times, but these words are gaining common currency, and the reader will want to understand them.

If my own neutrality and attempted objectivity are part of my attempt to make the readers think for themselves, the juxtaposition of conflicting viewpoints both within the secular and the religious approaches to an understanding of man are part of the same effort. Each position helps to raise issues about the validity of every other position. The reader himself must test these viewpoints against each other and against his own experience.

In the following chapters, apart from a presentation of various pictures of man in the popular culture and of my own viewpoint toward the end of the book, I have set out to examine some of the major views of man that have wielded a powerful influence in our time. Darwin, Marx, and Freud have had an enormous impact on our understanding of man and his society. In place of a discussion of Darwin's own thought, since he centered his attention largely upon the biological origins of man, I have chosen to present the thought of Julian Huxley, a contemporary who stands in the Darwinian tradition but gives a broader analysis of the human phenomenon. Marx and Freud remain as contemporaries. Over against these secular views of man I have included analyses of the thought of two Protestant thinkers (Kierkegaard and Niebuhr), one Roman Catholic (Teilhard de Chardin), and one Jew (Martin Buber). These men seem to me to have made four of the most impressive contributions to the understanding of man to be found in contemporary Western thought.

At the end of this book I have placed a short chapter that attempts to draw together many of the points made by each author whose work has been under consideration, raising in sharp focus some of the unanswered questions and the issues that still remain. Finally, in a concluding section of the book I have listed chapter by chapter a series of queries that are intended to help the individual reader or a discussion group toward critical reflection about the ideas presented in the chapter under study.

The original form of this work was written for an experimental program of study authorized by the Presbyterian Synod of Wisconsin. I am grateful to Harry Davis,

of Beloit College, and Gustav C. Nelson, of the First
Presbyterian Church, Beloit, Wisconsin, for their initial
invitation to prepare the earlier draft and for their com-
ments upon that form of the manuscript.

—Perry LeFevre

Chicago Theological Seminary

1: *Perspectives on Man in Popular Culture*

How do you perceive yourself? Do you think of yourself as strong or weak, as effective or ineffective, as liked by others or disliked? Would you characterize yourself as well-to-do or poor, in harmony with yourself or in inner conflict, anxious and hostile or kind and loving? Are you hard to get along with or easy? Self-perception is important. Psychotherapists know that one of the most important factors in sickness or in health is an individual's picture of himself. Change a man's picture of himself and you may be able to change the man. At the very least you will change his behavior.

What about others? How do you see your fellowmen— the man next door, the man in the slum or in the plush suburb, in distant India or Africa? Perceptions are important here too. They help to guide behavior. They determine action, whether we like it or not, whether they are accurate or not. So it is too with any generalized picture of man we have. It shapes our thinking and our action. Our generalized understanding of man interacts with and influences our view of ourselves, of the man next door, or of a person in India, just as the view we take of ourselves or of other particular men helps to shape our interpretation of human nature and destiny.

Many of the disagreements about political, economic, and social policy hinge on underlying conflicts about what man is and what he is meant to be. Perhaps more critical thinking about these underlying conflicts can help to disentangle and clarify the disagreements that seriously divide nations and groups within nations, preventing cooperation and forward movement. In any case such clarification may help us to test alternatives in understanding against human experience in ways that will expose inadequacies and lead to a reconstruction of our ideas about man.

At one time it was possible to speak of a fairly unified view of man in a given historical period or in a given culture. There was the classical view of man, the Christian view of man, the Renaissance view of man, the concept of man in Chinese thought, or the Vedic conception of man.[1] In our time no single view of man is dominant. There is confusion and a Babel of voices. Some of the views of man in the world today are vague but pervasive. They are expressed more at the level of feeling than of thought. They are latent in various cultural forms and remain uncriticized by most of us. Other views have been carefully worked out by thoughtful and scholarly men. They may be embodied in a whole system of ideas. It is difficult to be sure which kind of view has the greater influence. Certainly the popular views of man expressed in the mass culture have a great and unsuspected power over us, as T. S. Eliot suggested was the case with "the literature we read for amusement."[2] To the degree that this is true, it will be important to examine some of the views of man pervading the popular culture. They are promoted for profit by some, shared without full comprehension by many, and experienced by nearly all of us in America today. It will be well to have a critical look at the perspectives on man present in popular culture before we embark on our study of the views of some of the great interpreters of man in the present world.

I. The Detective Story

One of the very popular forms of recreational reading is the contemporary detective story. Studies of best sellers indicate that detective fiction leads every other category both in number of titles and in total sales. If we take seriously James D. Hart's judgment that the thoughts and feelings of the majority of a people are more accurately disclosed in the books on the best-seller lists than in the great books of a period, we may wish to make a careful study of the depiction of human existence they provide. "The volumes themselves may gather dust on library shelves," Hart writes, "but they have left a lasting impression on the American mind, etched deeply into a national consciousness."[3] Although the most popular writer of detective stories, and indeed of fiction in the twentieth century, is Erle Stanley Gardner (by 1955 Gardner had sales of over eighty-six million), in the 1950's Mickey Spillane led all others in the sales of individual titles. His latest paperback volume, *The Snake* (1964), shows that he has not lost his touch. The early analysis of Spillane's view of life made by Christopher La Farge is still accurate. Spillane's hero is one who mocks and flouts the law, both statutory and moral; he delights in assault and murder brutally executed. He is one who sits in personal judgment always above that of all other men. He is, says La Farge, essentially a character who is evil, sadistic, and immoral. Spillane's is a picture of sadism made into a way of life, a sadism that is held up as "a justifiable means to an admirable end."[4]

How different is Spillane's hero and the view of life he embodies from that of Agatha Christie's Hercule Poirot. Poirot is on the side not only of justice but of law, and people *matter* to him. Or again, if such a contrast be possible, compare Sherlock Holmes with Ian Fleming's hero James Bond. Two outlooks on life, two ways of understanding the nature of the evil that men do, and two modes of responding to the human situation. John Paterson, in his article "A Cosmic View of the Private Eye," has shrewdly contrasted the vision of the human situation which the two kinds of writing represent. The world of the transcendent sleuth can be penetrated by man's reason. Finally, the secrets must give way. But the world of the tough detective is open, dynamic, charged with fear and change. It is violent and irrational. Mind is not enough. Moreover, society itself is permeated with crime and guilt. Man is vicious and suffering in a perverted and amoral universe.[5]

What life is like is revealed not only in the figure of the hero but in the pattern of action involved. Charles J. Rolo has given an interesting explanation of the wide appeal of such detective fiction. He calls the detective story "modern man's Passion Play."

In the beginning is the murder, and the world is sorely out of joint. There appears the detective-hero and his foil, the latter representing the blindness of ordinary mortals—Dr. Watson, or the police, or, if the hero is a policeman, his bumbling associates. The detective is a man like the rest of us, with his share of human failings. . . . But this mortal has The Call—he is a Savior. In him is Grace, and we know that he will bring the Light.

The hero suspects everyone, for the murderer is Everyman; the murder is the symbol of guilt, the imperfection, that is in all of us. In his search for the hidden truth, the hero is exposed to danger, thrashes about in darkness, sometimes suffers in the flesh, for it is by his travail that the Savior looses the world of its sins. In the detective's hour of triumph, the world is, for a moment, redeemed. Unconsciously we die a little when the murderer meets his fate, and thus we are purged of guilt. We rejoice in the reassurance that beyond the chaos of life there is order and meaning. . . . We exult that Truth has been made known and that Justice has prevailed. All this the lowly who-dunit offers. And still that is not all.

By his personality, his deeds, his methods, the hero bears witness to a system of belief, a secular credo for a religious doctrine. He is the apostle of Science, like Holmes, or of Pure Reason, like Hercule Poirot. He may, like Maigret, believe that Understanding is the highest good and that its fruit is Compassion.[6]

II. The Mass Market Magazines

Detective fiction is not the only publishing phenomenon for mass consumption whose view of man raises interesting issues. Each month more than three million copies of *Playboy* are eagerly read by as many or more young men and women across the country. It has been claimed that 80 percent of its readers are between twenty and thirty-four years of age and the magazine is aimed at adolescents of all ages. *Playboy* today is a more complex publication than it was in its early years. Prosperity and success have greatly enriched its content by making it possible to include a wider variety of material, ranging from interviews with Martin Luther King and Nehru to an analysis of the cold war by Bertrand Russell. One issue even includes a lengthy panel discussion on leisure and automation much of which indirectly challenges the basic playboy philosophy.

Playboy's perspective on life is clearly revealed not so much in the pinups and cartoons, which might be found in other magazines designed for the college-age male, as in Hugh Hefner's editorializing, in such columns as the "Playboy Adviser," and in the advertising. Such material sets the context for a discussion of the *Playboy* view of man. The reader is urged to see himself as a happy hedonist, with woman as a play "thing." The identity needs of the late adolescent are to be resolved in an attitude of eat, drink, and "make Mary," for life can be a lot of fun. This fun philosophy promotes, of course, an incredibly simplified view of life and of man. Early in the magazine's history, and with reiteration, Hefner defined the playboy perspective:

He must see life not as a vale of tears, but as a happy time; he must take joy in his work, without regarding it as the end and all of living; he must be an alert man, a man of taste, a man who—without acquiring the stigma of the voluptuary or dilettante—can live life to the hilt. This is the sort of man we mean when we use the word *playboy*.[7]

"Living life to the hilt" appears to mean a self-centered pursuit of the pleasures afforded by an affluent society, the fashionable in clothes, food, and liquor, in theater, books, and music. Even more, "living life to the hilt" means for *Playboy* the pursuit of sex as fun. Underlying a good deal of the magazine's contents is a view of man as a sex-starved adolescent in Fantasyland. For all its variations on the theme, man is seen as one for whom the world and other people are for personal pleasure, and the focal pleasure is orgasm.

Fundamentally man is a consumer and his vocation is to manipulate events and people to maximize his own pleasurable consumption. This is life without commitment to anything more serious than providing conditions for succeeding moments of gratification, and gratification is understood in a simple and shallow way. In *Commentary*, Benjamin De Mott has described *Playboy*'s view as a "vision of the whole man reduced to his private parts."[8] Even some of the ads have a leer in them. *By George*, "a very persuasive fragrance for men," displays a darkened building with a lighted penthouse on top. The text reads: "She won't? *By George*, she will!" Fabergé advertises *Bedtime Perfume*: "Give her something beautiful to sleep in. *Bedtime Perfume* by Fabergé. This potent new potion needs only body warmth to work! So concentrated, three drops will wrap her in a fragrant glow that lasts the lovely night- or day-long."

If *Playboy* promotes a vastly oversimplified view of man for the college-age male and the young bachelors of America, other mass media carry out a similar function for the women. The total circulation of the confession magazines, for example, is about sixteen million. Their appeal is to a very different cultural level. George Gerbner reports that the confession magazine reader tends to accept the world as a chaotic and brutal place. She "feels that it is beyond her control. She feels that she is not an effective part of the broader society in which she lives."[9] She moves toward a kind of fatalism about life. Unlike the readers of the more prestigious women's magazines, who see their husbands as family oriented, for her the man is prominent and controlling. She must accept rough behavior in order to keep her man. Her obligations as wife are somewhat apart from her responsibility and emotions as mother.

The confession magazines present a picture of life in a reiterated plot line that speaks to these women's life and problems. The formula underlying most of the stories, according to Gerbner, might be summarized as follows:

A simple, trustful human is faced with a complex, real, and brutal world. Characters make their discovery of the truth by bumping up against troubles as they rush headlong down the path of least resistance. The overwhelming truth which they discover is that you must adjust. You must be set back—if necessary, beaten back—to the place where you were led into the sin of taking the line of least resistance, but this time you must accept necessity as a virtue. Therefore, you have learned what the publishers call the "truth"—the central lesson or moral of the story. Not only have ideals been pointed out as unrealistic but the most violent and hostile aspects of the reality of interpersonal and intrafamilial relationships have been asserted as the whole of them.

The path to happiness is a long and rocky path, and it goes through hell. The agony of the journey that is found in these stories is made possible only by the underlying assumption that life can be terrible. The reader assumes that the world is a hostile jungle, and the reader, identifying with the first-person narrator, travels this path and sins and suffers with the heroine as she stumbles inevitably into the booby trap of common nightmares that are placed along the road.[10]

To those who are infrequent readers of such publications, it might be said that in a sample of one hundred stories, one out of three involved serious physical illness, and one out of five, mental illness. There were seventeen fatal accidents, sixteen fistfights, fourteen murders, twelve violent quarrels, eight rapes, and four suicides. Some 44 percent of the narrators reported their own marriage on the point of breaking up and 21 percent recounted unpleasant scenes from childhood about the marital relationships of their parents.

Similar studies could indeed be made of the picture of life to be found in the women's service magazines (*Ladies' Home Journal, McCall's,* etc.). One recent report charts the radical shift in the portrayal of feminine life and the way to fulfillment. In the 1930's and early '40's the heroines of the stories were career women. They were individuals with strength of character—nurses, teachers, actresses, writers, saleswomen. By the end of 1949 only one of three heroines was a career woman. By 1959, writes Betty Friedan: "I went through issue after issue without finding a single heroine who had a career, a commitment to any work, art, profession, or mission in the world, other than 'Occupation Housewife.'" In a study of *McCall's,* for example, Mrs. Friedan found:

The image of woman that emerges . . . is young and frivolous, almost childlike, fluffy and feminine, passive; gaily content in a world of bedroom and kitchen, sex, babies and home.

The magazine surely does not leave out sex; the only passion, the only pursuit, the only goal a woman is permitted is the pursuit of a man. It is crammed full of food, clothing, cosmetics, furniture, and the physical bodies of young women, but where is the world of thought and ideas, the life of the mind and spirit? In the magazine image, women do no work except housework and work to keep their bodies beautiful and to get and keep a man.[11]

III. THE COMICS

Far broader in their appeal than even the most popular magazines and truly gigantic in their circulation are the comic strips. It has been estimated that four out of five Americans living in towns of over twenty-five hundred people read the comic strips, and if we include the number of readers in other countries, more than two hundred

million readers are followers of one or more of the strips.
What kind of picture of human existence does such a popular art form paint? Though the form of the art is simple,
and the vision of life simplified as it must be for all mass
consumption media, there may be more diversity in the
comics than in the other types of popular culture we have
considered. There is a greater range in the life situations
that are depicted, for comics are made to appeal to all
ages and classes and the artist-writers themselves seem to
possess a greater diversity of viewpoint as well. From simple depictions of everyday domesticity in *Gasoline Alley*
to the social satire of *Li'l Abner* and *Pogo,* there is an immense distance. Equally great is the distance between the
vision of life promoted by Harold Gray in *Little Orphan
Annie* and that expressed by Charles M. Schulz's *Peanuts.*
Annie clearly gives voice to a right-wing social philosophy
in which from time to time its author has advocated "the
abolition of unions, impeachment of a president (Franklin
Delano Roosevelt), capital punishment, and the establish-
ment of an oligarchy in this country."[12] After a study of the
strip for one hundred and ten weeks, one analyst summed
up what he found:

> *Little Orphan Annie* presents a picture of the world about
> us as many see it, one in which the hard-working captains of
> industry struggle against a vicious and uncompromising under-
> ground in order to protect capitalism, earn large profits and
> thus assume their social responsibilities, i.e., be charitable to
> the needy.[13]

Daddy Warbucks himself, much like Mickey Spillane,
likes to take the law into his own hands, justified only by
what he believes to be the moral superiority of his way of
life and his own power.

Quite different is the vision of life discoverable in *Peanuts*. Much has been written about Schulz's strip, but nothing more penetrating has been said than the little book by Robert L. Short, *The Gospel According to Peanuts*. Short finds Schulz's understanding of human existence deeply Christian. Whether their creator consciously intended it or not, the various strips communicate the basic Christian understanding of life indirectly. Certainly Schulz, who is an active Christian layman, expresses his own understanding of the meaning of life, whether or not he has set out explicitly to teach the Christian message. Indeed, he says: "If you do not say anything in a cartoon, you might as well not draw it at all. Humor which does not say anything is worthless humor. So I contend that a cartoonist must be given a chance to do his own preaching."[14]

The mass media play upon the minds and feelings of all of us continuously. Only a few of the pictures of man —of human existence—have been examined here. Radio and TV, movies and popular music, surely play their part too in shaping and forming our thought and feelings about other people and about ourselves. An individual who has read *Little Orphan Annie* uncritically for thirty years is surely just as much shaped in his viewpoint as another individual who has spent an equal amount of time with the Bible. But views of man are even more effectively embodied in the attitudes of cultural and class groups. A white man brought up in certain parts of the South, an individual spending his early years within a particular ethnic group, a typical middle-class American, is likely to absorb without knowing it at the time certain assumptions about himself and about other men. The racist attitudes of Governor Wallace, the teaching and nonviolent action

of Martin Luther King, as well as the politicoeconomic
philosophies of extremist groups like the John Birch
Society or the Communist Party, incorporate divergent
understandings of man that lead to radically different
versions of the good society and communal life.

Whatever the implicit views of man we have absorbed
from our culture and from the mass media, or elsewhere,
our behavior is likely to be guided by them. They are part
of our world of assumptions by which we gauge other
people's actions and attitudes. They are part of our picture
of ourselves, for our self-image reflects the appraisals we
think others are making of us.

But implicit views of man may be quite false. They may
be distorted, or oversimple, or only half-truths about man.
We need to be aware of these pictures of man which are
present in our culture. We need to evaluate and criticize
them. Such awareness, evaluation, and criticism are possible, however, only if we have clarified our own view of
man. We need an articulated body of understanding to
set over against the many alternative views that contend
for acceptance and loyalty.

One of the ways to develop a critical understanding of
man's nature, condition, and destiny is to examine some of
the carefully worked out views of man offered by the
major thinkers of the contemporary world. We would need
to set these views side by side, to compare them, to let
them raise questions for each other. Such comparison is
important for appraising their claimed relevance and adequacy, but even more, it may help us to develop our own
constructive interpretation.

Few, if any, of the carefully worked out theories of
man's existence are purely descriptive and analytical. They
are usually normative and evaluative as well. Though they

try to tell us something about what man is, they contain a thesis or several theses about what man *ought* to be. It becomes possible, therefore, to organize most theories about man around three central questions or themes: First, a theory of man usually carries the assumption, Something is wrong with man; it usually carries an answer to the question, What is wrong with man? Second, such a theory also contains a normative judgment—a view of what man ought to be or could be. That is, a second central motif has to do with the nature of human fulfillment, with what the *good* man is. Finally, a third theme has to do with the way of moving from what is wrong with man to what man is "meant to be" or to what his fulfillment as man is.

For example, today we live in a world that is permeated by psychological categories. Men tend to look at one another and use psychological concepts to describe what they see. The psychologist may look at a man, or the layman using psychological categories may look at him, and conclude: "He's not adjusted"; "he's not fully functioning"; or "he's not actualizing himself." If the difficulty is more serious and the individual is something of a problem to himself and to others, he may say, "That man's neurotic." Or if something still more serious is wrong with the individual, so much so that he is out of touch with reality, or cannot get along in the community, or if he is dangerous to himself and to others, he may be labeled a "psychotic."

Any such diagnosis as to what is wrong with man depends upon some assumptions as to what adjustment or healthy functioning are. The goal may be described as full-functioning or emotional maturity. Christian theology has parallel categories to describe the human condition and the fulfillment of man. What is wrong with man is that he is a sinner; he is in "unfaith." He has separated himself from God and from his fellowmen. The goal for man is faith, forgiveness, followed by growth in grace, by love and hope and the gifts of the Spirit.

From the psychological perspective the way from what is wrong to the goal may be termed conditioning, education, reeducation, therapy. From the theological perspective the way will be faith. But faith is a gift from God. Man is finally saved or healed by God. He does not save himself. He is not healed by his own good works.

In succeeding chapters of this book we will examine a number of carefully worked out understandings of man, using these three focal issues for our framework of analysis. One of the issues the reader should keep in mind is whether the different answers to these fundamental questions (What is wrong with man? What is human fulfillment? What is the way?) are really different answers, or whether they merely use different language to express the same thing. And when real differences are discovered, we need to ask what the roots of these differences are. Do they lie in a different way of looking at the world? Are they the result of the neglect of certain elements in the human situation by one type of observer? We need also to try to discover the implications that follow from such differences.

2: *Julian Huxley—*
Man in Evolution—
A Humanist View

Sɪʀ Jᴜʟɪᴀɴ Hᴜxʟᴇʏ is a distinguished English biologist. He was born in London, on June 22, 1887, the grandson of T. H. Huxley, who was famous for his part in the Darwinian controversy in the late nineteenth century, and the brother of the novelist Aldous Huxley. He was educated at Eton and Balliol College, Oxford. He was a Fellow of New College, Oxford, and in 1925 was appointed Professor of Zoology in King's College, London University. From 1935 to 1942, Huxley was Secretary of the Zoological Society of London, and between 1946 and 1948 he was Director General of UNESCO. Huxley has lectured widely both in England and in America. He has written a number of books, both technical and popular, winning the Kalinga Prize for Distinguished Popular Writing in Science.

As a biologist and specialist in evolutionary biology, Professor Huxley might be expected to look at man in the light of his own discipline. But Huxley has not limited himself to any narrowly conceived view of man as an organism; rather, he has offered a full-bodied interpretation of man's nature and destiny, projected onto the background of a wide-ranging description of the nature of evolution itself.

I. Huxley's Conception of Evolution

A. *The Three Levels of Evolution*

The dominance of evolutionary thinking in all that Huxley has to say about man demands some summary of what he has to say about evolution itself. For Huxley, nature—all of it—is a single process of evolution. By evolution he means "a self-operating, self-transforming process which in its course generates both greater variety and higher levels of organization."[1] Though it is a single process, evolution is constituted by three subprocesses: the first cosmic, the second biological, and the third psychosocial.

At the cosmic level, operating by simple physical and chemical interaction, the tempo of change is very slow. Only limited variety and a low level of organization are achieved. The biological level of transformation is what we ordinarily think of as evolutionary process. We know this level of organization only on the earth, but it is probable that it goes on elsewhere in the universe as well. Evolution at the biological level operates through self-reproduction and self-variation of organic matter, giving rise to natural selection as a method of self-transformation. There is a differential reproduction of variants. That is, variations are produced, but some survive and some do not, according to their success in adapting to their total environment. At higher levels of biological process mental activities develop.

The third, or psychosocial phase of evolution, operates at the level of the transformation of culture. There is a self-production and self-variation of mind and its products. Enormously more complex levels of organization are achieved. Furthermore, each higher level not only represents an increased tempo of change but also affects the lower phases of the evolutionary process, conditioning and even determining aspects of their own transformation.

It is important for our understanding of Huxley's view to grasp something of the inner changes involved in evolutionary process at the biological level, and of the time spans represented by all aspects of the process. First let us look at the time spans as they might be roughly estimated. Our galaxy is perhaps four or five thousand million years old. Life originated about two thousand million years ago. Man had his beginnings five thousand years ago. Using a more dramatic illustration, Huxley cites Sir James Jeans's example of the obelisk, Cleopatra's Needle. If we let this monument (sixty-nine feet high) represent the time lapse since the origin of life to the time of man's beginning, then the amount of time since man emerged on the scene would be represented by the thinness of a postage stamp.

If one wants to generalize what has taken place at the biological level in evolution, he can say that a succession of organizational types has appeared, the later ones having a higher level of organization than the earlier:

Structural organization rises from the pre-cellular to the cellular and the multi-cellular; there follows the multi-tissued type, like the sea-anemone, and then the multi-organed type like the worm or the mollusk or the early anthropod. The multi-organed animal attains new mechanical and physiological levels, as in crustacea and fish, new and superior modes of organization and reproduction as in insects and reptiles, and new levels of behavior appear, as in birds and mammals and social insects. New methods of integration and homeostatic adjustment arise, such as the endocrine system and the temperature-regulating mechanism of the higher vertebrates.[2]

One after another, there is a succession of dominant types, each in turn supplanted by a later type which, because of its improvements, takes over the dominant position. A great majority of evolutionary trends are intrinsically limited. They stabilize or come to a dead end, or are obliterated. Though the lines of major biological improvement seem to have exhausted themselves, in man new possibilities of evolutionary advance emerged at the psychosocial level, and a new method of advance beyond natural selection begins to play a part. It is this new method which fashions the means of man's destiny, but it is the total evolutionary thrust which defines its general character. For Huxley the crucial fact about evolution is not that it is change, but that this change seen in its widest perspective includes progress.

B. *The Question of "Progress"*

It is just here that a very important distinction must be made if we are to understand Huxley accurately. Evolution includes progress, but not all that goes on in the evolutionary process is progressive. Evolution includes retrogression, blind alleys, arrest of development, and destruction as well as progress. The notion of progress is, however, one of the keys to understanding Huxley's interpretation of human destiny and his sometimes explicit and sometimes implicit norms for evaluating human institutions and activity. It is further important to understand what Huxley means by the term "progress," since there are many who would deny that either biological evolution or cultural evolution are or can be progressive.

What are the criteria of progress, according to Huxley? In the inorganic sector the one criterion is complexity of organization. In the organic phase, complexity increases, but other criteria are important: first, the capacity to control and be independent of changes in the environment, and then the degree of capacity for knowledge, emotion, and purpose, and especially the capacity for learning from experience. All these criteria are still involved at the human level, but new ones are to be added, namely, increased understanding and attainment of intrinsic values. For Huxley, there is then a higher and lower, a standard of measurement implicit in evolutionary process, and a progressive directional movement within the process.

As against earlier doctrines of progress one might well wonder whether Huxley considers the future of progressive movement secure. On this question his answer is qualified. He believes progress is *probably* inevitable— "for some considerable evolutionary future"—but he does not believe that it is inevitable in the sense that it must be either steady or universal. There may well be retrogression here and there, and relative advance here rather than there. "But given the present state of the human race, its thirst for knowledge and betterment and the extent of its accumulated tradition, I regard it as certain that some degree of progress will for some time inevitably continue to occur."[3]

Evolution, seen in the dimension of progress, represents human destiny. It defines the character of man's future task—of what he should work for and believe in, and of what becomes increasingly possible for him if he does work for it and believe in it. Whatever is wrong with man or with human institutions is what obstructs, impedes, or resists progress. Whatever is good about man and human institutions is good to the degree that it supports and nourishes this directional movement, this movement toward the increase and fulfillment of human possibilities.

"The most important of all the prerequisites for future progress," writes Huxley, "is the acceptance of the fact of progress, and the understanding of its nature; for we cannot expect to achieve what we do not believe in."[4]

II. The Role of Man

We will have to look carefully at Huxley's sketch of what is called for if we are to have progress, if man is to realize his destiny. First, however, let us examine his view of the uniqueness of man and his place in nature, which makes progress possible at the human level of existence.

The distinctive feature of man, Huxley believes, is that he is a cultural animal. Of course he has distinguishing biological characteristics, but what differentiates him sharply from other animals is culture. "Culture" here means that man has patterns of language and law, ritual and belief, art and skill, ideas and technology. All these cultural patterns are learned. They depend upon symbols for their communication. They are not innate. They do not, as do animal reactions, depend upon sign stimuli for their release.

The components of culture are finally symbolic. They are the result of man's capacity for abstraction, generalization, creative imagination, and systematization. Man can construct organized patterns of conscious experience, thought, and purpose.

Some other writers have said that the distinguishing character of man is to be found in rational thought and in language as its instrument. Huxley takes a much broader view, with important consequences. He would hold that a narrow emphasis on the intellectual takes no account of man's emotional and aesthetic capacities. It neglects intuition and imagination, and consequently does not give recognition to the important role of arts and skills, rituals and religious experiences, in distinctively human evolution. A comprehensive view of man's special characteristics would take them into account and be concerned to show their influence on cultural evolution.

Huxley designedly uses the term "noetic" (derived from the Greek word for mind) to describe all these areas of human mental activity. He would include "all kinds of conscious experience and activity, rational intellect and imagination, emotionally motivated beliefs and attitudes, mystical experiences and aesthetic expressions, deliberate technical skills and symbolic ritual actions."[5]

It is this noetic dimension which distinguishes man from the rest of the animals, and it is in this dimension that future evolution will take place. "Man's evolution is not biological but psychosocial; it operates by the mechanism of cultural tradition, which involves the cumulative self-reproduction and self-variation of mental activities and their products."[6]

Man has a cosmic office. He is called to be the instrument of the evolutionary process on this planet, "the sole agent capable of effecting major advances and of realizing new possibilities for evolving life."[7] Says Huxley: "Man's destiny, his duty and privilege in one, is to continue in his own person the advance of the cosmic process of evolution."[8] It is as if he had suddenly been "appointed managing director of the biggest business of all."[9]

III. The Conditions of Progress

Evolution at the human level takes place, then, in and through the culture. It is man's to promote and guide. But such promotion and guidance of the evolutionary process depends on an understanding of the conditions of progressive change within the culture.

For Huxley the two most important conditions for pro-

gressive cultural change seem to be the increase of knowledge and the interpenetration and interaction of cultures.
Interaction between cultures makes possible the orchestra-
tion of human diversity from competitive discord to har-
monious symphony. The phrase "makes possible" should
doubtless be underlined, since Huxley is not so naïve as
to believe that interaction necessarily has such a result.
But whereas in biological evolution the types are condemned to remain distinct, resulting in permanent competitive coexistence or dominance of one and reduction
or extinction of the other, such a result is not necessary
within cultural evolution. Man not only has a self-repro-
ducing tradition, but the possibilities of communication
enable different traditions to enrich one another. Culture
is, in fact, for Huxley, "a self-maintaining system or organization of intercommunicating human beings and their
products, or if we wish to be a little more precise, of the
results of the intercommunication of the minds of human
individuals in society."[10]

But the increase of knowledge is also an important key
to psychosocial evolution—partly of course because it is
tied to the fact of the intercommunication of cultures, for
knowledge and the implications of newly discovered
knowledge for the rest of culture can be quickly spread
beyond its point of origin.

Of course, the increase of knowledge helps man to
handle the practical problems of life more effectively—
health, food, housing, etc. But for Huxley the most significant results of the increase of knowledge are (a) the fact
that it is the result of a reliable *method* for acquiring
knowledge; (b) the fact that it makes possible a true understanding of man's place in the history of life and the
world, and of the conditions necessary for his fulfillment;

and (c) that in consequence of (b) it necessitates the criticism of older ideological systems that have interpreted the nature and destiny of man and the creation of a new synthesis—an ideology that will be both an expression of evolutionary progress at the human level and an instrument for pushing progress still farther.

IV. Huxley's Belief: Evolutionary Humanism

A. *The New Synthesis*

Huxley calls his anticipated new synthesis "the evolutionary vision," or "transhumanism," or sometimes simply "humanism." An actual synthesis that could serve as the organizing ideology for a world culture consciously oriented to progress awaits a new "prophet"; or at least it will take a long time to construct on the basis of shared efforts of many. But Huxley believes that some of the main lines of its shape are clear, and its implications in criticism of earlier syntheses can be stated. Much of Huxley's non-scientific writing has been devoted to his effort to state the criticisms, outline the need for a new synthesis, and suggest some of the factors that he believes must be included in the new interpretation of reality.

Since the criticisms arise out of Huxley's positive convictions, it may be well to state the most important of these. One of the most important of Huxley's theses is that nature is a unified evolutionary process. We have already reviewed certain aspects of this thesis, but the critical implications need to be stated. One is that all (1) forms of dualism are false, including the dualisms of nature and supernature, body and spirit, the actual and the ideal, matter and mind. Another is that there is no fixity; there (2.) is only change, and change is directional. The positive implication is that we must develop modes of unitary thinking; we must develop "process" modes of thought; we must, since process is always relative, reject all absolutistic modes of thought. We shall indicate in more specific terms the kind of change such thinking implies for religion, politics, economics, and art. But it will be well first to see why such changed thinking is so important for Huxley.

B. *The Importance of Beliefs*

For Huxley, ideas, beliefs, theories, concepts, forms of language, are important. The raw material of experience does not come to us organized. Experience is organized anew in each one of us. Linguistic and other forms organize and synthesize the sense data streaming in upon us. Consequently the language, the ideas, the concepts, and belief systems available to us in our culture, and selectively appropriated by us as individuals, become the means of interpreting our presented world. We see, feel, and know our world through these means. Certain kinds of words and concepts may prevent us from seeing or comprehending what others may see or know. They may distort our perception, give us false signals.

Men need not just ideas and concepts and language to organize their world; they also need belief systems. Every human being and every society is faced with "three overshadowing questions: What am I, or what is man? What is the world in which I find myself, or what is the environment which man inhabits? And what is my relation to the world, or what is man's destiny?"[11] Man cannot direct the course of his life until he has some sort of answer to these questions. A belief system, or as Huxley sometimes calls it, a "noetic integrator" (an ideology, a religion) is necessary. Beliefs are essentially dynamic for Huxley. They give "an orientation to potential action and a directional set to personality and to society."[12]

If man would release human potentiality, if he is to nurture progress, his belief system must be soundly built on the most accurate knowledge he has. His new belief system will displace earlier schemes that served the same function. For example, his new religion must discard certain aspects of earlier religious conceptions—the distinction between natural and supernatural, the traditional notions of God and revelation. But religion is important. It is all-important when its functions are understood, for it is exactly the all-encompassing "noetic integrator" that embodies the answer to the question of man's nature and destiny. Moreover, the sense of the sacred or of the holy, the qualities of mystery, religious experience, and "spiritual development" are not to be neglected. They represent the height of human potentiality. They are real and of great importance, but their interpretation can no longer be given along traditional lines.

Similarly, other aspects of man's life are not to be neglected or explained away. The function of the artist, for example, "is to bear witness to the variety and the richness of reality, and to express it effectively and significantly in terms related to the life and aims of man."[13] Art provides a qualitative enrichment of life by creating a diversity of new experience. Creative expression "can act both as a liberating and as an integrative force in the developing human creature."[14]

C. Relevance for Practical Problems

But the new belief system Huxley calls for has implications for the "practical" affairs of men as well. Population says Huxley, is a problem of our age. We need the most drastic reversal of our thinking as the result of the population explosion. The tremendous increase in the quantity of people "is increasingly affecting the quality of their lives and their future, and affecting it almost wholly for the worse."[15] The population explosion raises the whole issue, "What are people for?"[16] And the answer of Huxley's evolutionary vision has to do with their quality as human beings. We must sharply reduce the rate of population growth if we are not to exceed the resources needed to nurture human fulfillment.

Similarly Huxley believes the "consumption explosion" leads to an overexploitation of resources that is essentially self-defeating. An economic system that depends on an ever-increasing stimulation of the number of human wants wastes resources that ought to be used for the promotion of qualitative human achievement. Quantitative approaches may be made to the satisfaction of elementary human needs. Beyond that point, the sheer emphasis on increasing quantitative consumption not only may waste resources but may reduce qualitative human achievement.[17]

Politically and culturally, Huxley believes that his evolutionary humanism could provide the basis for healing the breach between East and West, between Communism and anti-Communism. The state becomes, in his view, "an organization to facilitate and promote the development of its members and the fullest realization of their individual potentialities."[18] And the task of the great powers such as the United States is to give the leadership that will facilitate the transformation of the world "to higher minimum standards of material life for the underprivileged and more freedom for the exploited and the backward," thus "providing the necessary foundation" for the further release of human potentiality.[19]

Evolutionary humanism, as a "religion," a belief system, or a noetic integrator is then one of the major instruments for carrying on the evolutionary process itself at the human cultural level. Huxley believes that this philosophy rightly understands man's nature and destiny, and by giving man this understanding it increases his capacity to realize his destiny. Destiny is alternatively described as being an instrument of progress or the actualization of potentiality.

V. OVERCOMING OBSTACLES TO PROGRESS

What, according to Huxley, stands in the way of man's realization of his destiny? One of the major obstacles, which we have already discussed in another fashion, is the lack of an adequate belief system. Man's culture is divided by a multiplicity of belief systems, many of which are in conflict with one another. Further, at some levels of the culture the older belief systems that have given man direction and confidence have been eroded or displaced, and no new vision has replaced them. Huxley, of course, believes that his humanist vision is an answer to just this problem.

Though the general tone of Huxley's writing is optimistic, he recognizes that there are difficulties. In his Darwin centennial address he lists the challenging monsters in our evolutionary path: the threat of superscientific war—nuclear, chemical, and biological; the threat of overpopulation; the rise and appeal of Communist ideology; the failure to bring China into the UN; the overexploitation of natural resources; the erosion of the world's cultural variety; our concern with means and not ends and with quantity, not quality. Huxley declares that though these are great problems, especially if we deal with them piece-meal, they can perhaps be dealt with successfully if they are seen as symptoms of a new evolutionary situation that requires a new organization of thought—i.e., Huxley's evolutionary humanism.

Unlike some thinkers who have believed in progress, Huxley admits "the basic fact of the evil in human nature (including the intellectual evils of stupidity and error, and the spiritual evil of self-righteousness)."[20] He repudi-ates, at least upon occasion, a view that ascribes such evil entirely to social conditions.[21] Evil is not described as original sin. The meaning of evil lies in its destructiveness or restrictiveness, as over against the positive and con-structive "forces" in individual and society. On the one hand, there are such forces as "hate, envy, despair, fear, destructive rage and aggressiveness, restrictive selfishness in all its forms, from greed to lust for power"; there is internal disharmony, frustration, and unresolved conflict. On the other hand, there is "comprehension, love in the broadest sense . . . , the urge to creation and fuller expres-sion, the desire to feel useful in contributing to some larger enterprise or purpose, pure enjoyment and the cultivation of intrinsic talents and capacities, and that constructive disposition of forces that we may call inner harmony."[22]

Man, who is the only agent for realizing life's further progress, is also the main obstacle to its realization. Man, who can control and utilize external nature through his understanding, must "now learn to understand, control and utilize the forces of his own nature." "This applies as much to the blind urge to reproduction as to personal greed or desire for power, as much to arrogance and fanaticism, whether nationalist or religious, as to sadism or self-indulgence."[23]

Huxley's most frequent example of how man might make progress in understanding and controlling himself has to do with the phenomenon of guilt. Most men feel guilt; these feelings can be destructive. Freud has helped us understand how man's conscience is formed and how guilt feelings arise. Using this understanding, he seems to be saying, man can reconcile the conflicts among impulse, social demand, the ideal. Such a reconciliation will involve the relationship between individual, personal development, and the long-term progressive realization of the possibilities for man—social evolution. The individual will see these two coming together in some fashion. The individual is to fulfill his own highest possibilities; finally, he is to undergo that kind of development which leaves the way permanently open for fresh possibilities of growth and which will be his contribution to the realization of the larger goal.

Such understanding of the relation between the individual and the social is what is disclosed in the vision of evolutionary humanism. Will such a vision be understood? Will it be appropriated? Will men be loyal to it? Huxley's answer:

What I am sure of is that some such naturalistic and evolutionary synthesis as I have indicated is inevitable, and that if the resultant view of human destiny is essentially true, it will prevail.[24]

Whatever men's response to it, Huxley does not believe that this view offers any panaceas:

Human and other evolutionary situations are multicausal; they depend on complex and largely autonomous processes, not just on fixed and calculable mechanisms. All organisms and all evolutionary situations are complex patterns involving many kinds of elements. Accordingly, any resultant characteristic will always be in the nature of a compromise, involving a balance between different needs, between different selective pressures.[25]

Nevertheless, so far as the vision itself is concerned, he holds that "beliefs are ultimately subject to necessity; in the long run man cannot believe what is false; . . . truth will eventually prevail."[26]

3: *Teilhard de Chardin —*
Man in Evolution —
A Christian View

TEILHARD DE CHARDIN, 1881–1955, distinguished pale-
ontologist and French Jesuit, whose church forbade
the publication of his books during his lifetime, has, since
his death, met an amazing response from Catholics, Prot-
estants, and nonbelievers. Several hundred thousand
copies of his works are already in print in English. New
books discussing Teilhard's thought are flooding the market; new translations are appearing each year; and there
still remain numerous unpublished manuscripts to be
edited.

Friend of Julian Huxley, and sharing many of the same
views on the nature of the evolutionary process, Teilhard
sought to provide a Christian interpretation of evolution.
The roots of Teilhard's Christian evolutionism go back
on the one hand to an interest in geology formed during
adolescence and on the other to the informal study of
paleontology begun when he taught in a Jesuit college
in Egypt. He began his formal study of paleontology in
Paris after his ordination to the priesthood and just before
the First World War, continuing after the war until he
took his doctorate in 1922. Teilhard seems to have re-

mained a believer in the traditional idea of Creation until about 1908. From that time on, in his studies and in his fieldwork on expeditions in China, Africa, and South America, he gave himself to developing a synthetic vision of the world and of man in the world which would hold together a scientific approach to nature and the development of mankind, with a religious, indeed with a Christian, interpretation of the meaning of these phenomena. Not only was Teilhard uniquely equipped for this task, for he became both a distinguished scientist and a sensitive religious spirit as well, but as a member of the two communities, he wanted to speak to and for both.

I. TEILHARD'S INTENTION AND METHOD

Though Teilhard was both a scientist and a man of faith, he tried to distinguish clearly between the views he held on scientific grounds and those which he derived from his religious faith. The obvious reason for this effort was that he wished to gain a hearing from his scientific colleagues and from secularized men and women. A second important consideration, however, was his desire to avoid conflict with the religious interpretations sanctioned by his church. In much of his work, therefore, Teilhard uses what he calls a *phenomenological method*. What he wants to do is to look at the phenomena—the appearances—or the events as they appear, not to delve beneath the surface of events to discover some kind of deeper explanation for why things are as they are. In 1942, for example, he wrote in a preface to an important unpublished essay on man: "Discussing scientific perspectives as a scientist I must and shall restrict myself to the investigation of the arrangement of appearances, that is of 'phenomena.' Since my concern is with their connections and with the succession manifested by these phenomena, I shall not deal with their underlying causalities."[1] Again and again Teilhard disclaimed the writing of metaphysics or theology in his interpretation of evolution. He wished to avoid the condemnation or criticism of his views by the church, and he wished to claim the attention of the secular scientific world which he felt might well reject all he had to say if they thought he was importing nonobservable elements into his view of evolution. In the preface to his most important work, *The Phenomenon of Man,* he wrote:

If this book is to be properly understood, it must be read not as a work on metaphysics, still less as a sort of theological essay, but purely and simply as a scientific treatise. The title itself indicates that. This book deals with man *solely* as a phenomenon; but it also deals with the *whole* phenomenon of man.[2]

There are, of course, other essays in which Teilhard explicitly attempts to bring a Christian understanding to bear on the phenomena that he has described and analyzed as a scientist, and these works, too, are an important part of Teilhard's view of man. His understanding of man was finally a unity, a synthesis of his insights as a scientist and as a Christian.

II. Evolution—A New Context for Thought

Teilhard believed that a decisive alteration had occurred in man's view of himself and his world through the discovery of evolution. Our temporal view of the world differs radically from that of our ancestors. We have come to see "that every constituent element of the world (whether of a being or a phenomenon) has of necessity emerged from that which preceded it," and that "the threads or chains of elements thus formed" represent a "naturally ordered series in which the links" cannot be exchanged, and "that no elemental thread in the Universe is wholly independent in its growth of its neighboring threads."[3]

The human phenomenon is thus placed within a new context. If "everything is the sum of its past" and if "nothing is comprehensible except through its history," then the meaning of the human phenomenon can be elucidated only in relation to its past.[4] What man is and what he is to be can be read only in relation to his history, and his history can be understood only as it is interwoven with the whole temporal context. Many of those who have looked at the whole temporal context from what they believed to be a scientific point of view have seen only change or process. They have chosen to remain agnostic concerning direction, or have introduced metaphysical or religious perspectives in order to claim that direction was implicit in the process. Teilhard believes that, while metaphysical or religious understanding may support the notion that the world process has direction, such a claim can be established on scientific grounds alone. The view that the whole process taken as events open to perception discloses a direction or an *axis* along which the process moves Teilhard believes is supported by the facts.

A. *Toward Increasingly Centered Complexity*

This axis, or direction, is one from beginning to end, but it takes different forms at each new phase of the development that is evolution. In the first phase, the development of the cosmos, the movement is in the direction of increasingly centered complexity. In the course of time there is an increasing combination of simple elements, ever more tightly organized among themselves. There is an increase of complexity "not only in the number and diversity of the elements included in each case, but at least as much in the number and correlative variety of links formed between these elements."[5] Electrons are formed into atoms, atoms into molecules, molecules into living cells, and so on. Moreover, arranged according to a scale of complexity, the elements are seen to succeed one another in the historical order of their birth.

B. *Toward Consciousness*

The more complex a being is, "the more it is centered upon itself and therefore the more *aware* does it become."[6] This clue leads Teilhard to the second form in which the single axis or direction is expressed. He coins the terms "cephalization" and "cerebralization" to express what he sees happening. From the "lowest to the highest level of the organic world there is a persistent and clearly defined thrust of animal forms toward species with more sensitive and elaborate nervous systems."[7] Teilhard believes that this change can be observed in the insects as well as in the vertebrates, that it is disclosed among the vertebrates from class to class, order to order, family to family. Among mammals—the ungulates, the carnivores, and especially the primates—as time passes, the brain grows more complex. Thus the axis of centered complexity takes on a new form in the growth of consciousness.

C. *Toward Human Fulfillment*

Within the span of human history a third form of single directional movement develops. Human life has been growing in complexity and in consciousness during the span of human history. *Now* it does so in the social and cultural dimension. Where earlier evolution went on more or less automatically without the conscious awareness and influence of its participants, now within the sphere of human life evolution is directly influenced by reflective activity and the future is the direct result of human reflective activities. The fact that man can think about his world and anticipate the future means that he can, if he has the will, direct his own evolution, up to a certain point at least.

If we examine Teilhard's view of the human scene more closely, we find, first, that the sphere of evolution is now social and cultural. Life becomes ever more complex and conscious at the social and cultural levels. What has happened in the thirty thousand years of human history from the caveman to the present is an almost unbelievable advance in what Teilhard calls *concentration*: "economic concentration, manifest in the unification of the earth's energies; intellectual concentration, manifest in the unification of our knowledge in a coherent system (science); social concentration, manifest in the unification of the human mass as a thinking whole."[8] Social organization has grown more and more complex through the process of collectivization.

"We see," says Teilhard, "Nature combining molecules and cells in the living body to construct separate individuals, and the same Nature, stubbornly pursuing the same course but on a higher level, combining individuals in social organisms to obtain a higher order of psychic results."[9] In the case of man the rapid psychic rise takes the form of "the growth of a collective memory," "the development, through the increasingly rapid transmission of thought, of what is in effect a generalized nervous system, emanating from certain defined centres and covering the entire surface of the globe," "the growth through the interaction and ever-increasing concentration of individual viewpoints, of a faculty of common vision penetrating beyond the continuous and static world of popular conception into a fantastic but still manageable world of atomized energy."[10]

This growth of a kind of envelope of consciousness Teilhard calls the "noosphere." "What is really going on, under cover and in the form of human collectivization, is the super-organization of Matter upon itself which as it continues to advance produces its habitual specific effect, the further liberation of consciousness."[11]

Evolution at the human level is to be differentiated from earlier forms of evolution not only because it occurs in relation to social structures and culture on which man's conscious activity has a direct influence but also because at the human level man becomes conscious of the process of evolution itself. "The basic characteristic of Man," says Teilhard, "the root of all his perfections, is his gift of awareness in the second degree. Man not only knows; he knows that he knows."[12] The significance of this fact is that man can now know what it is that he is a part of; his reflection will make a clear difference about the future. Evolution, at the human level, is, so to say, in his hands. Knowing his past and present, man can give direction to his future. And knowing man's past and present, Teilhard believes that he himself can with some confidence predict the future.

Even apart from his religious convictions, Teilhard believes that there is ample ground for optimism about man's future. The direction of evolution disclosed in the development of the cosmos, the development of life, and now in the history of man will, he thinks, sustain the expectation that evolution now moves toward human fulfillment.

Otherwise, what has gone before would be pointless and the realms of nature and history absurd. Since there is direction up through the present—though much which seems to be waste and much suffering and evil may have been involved—there is no ground at the level of appearances or phenomena for holding with Sartre that there is only absurdity or with Heidegger that the end is death. Nevertheless, Teilhard does believe that the future is not predetermined and closed. Man has freedom; necessity does not rule. He sees three possible options before man. We stand at the crossroads.

The first choice facing man is between pessimism and optimism. The question is: "Is the Universe utterly pointless, or are we to accept that it has a meaning, a future, a purpose?"[13] For those who choose pessimism, only one course is possible: "a refusal to go further; desertion which is equivalent to turning back." For those who see the value of Being, there are two alternatives. On the one hand, there are those who would hold that the more we try to organize and know the world, the more we move closer together and into bondage. They would see breaking the bonds that confine us as the only way to a state of higher Being. Theirs is the way of asceticism, withdrawal, mysticism. This is the path taken by Oriental wisdom and by a number of Christians. But the other way is that of those who are "faithful to Earth"; they are the "believers in some ultimate value in the tangible evolution of things."[14]

There is still another division within the last group. There are those who believe that man should move toward individualism and pluralism and those who believe he should move toward community and union. The former find that they can only achieve the desired uniqueness and personal freedom in opposition to others, while they see collectivism and totalitarianism as the result of movements

toward unity. For the others, like Teilhard himself, totalitarianism is a temporary aberration of the movement
toward unity. The unification of man, society, and culture
finally leads toward personalization, toward increased
differentiation, and to a richer fulfillment for the individual. There are only four possibilities then: "to cease to act,
by some form of suicide; to withdraw through a mystique
of separation; to fulfil ourselves individually by egotisti-
cally segregating ourselves from the mass; or to plunge
resolutely into the stream of the whole in order to become
a part of it."[15] Each of these ways corresponds to a vision
of what the universe really is and what evolution itself
really is. One view must be true and the others false.
Teilhard believes that direction or meaning *is* disclosed,
that there is a pattern which shows increasing complexity,
then increasing consciousness, and finally a "reflexion" in
which consciousness moves upon itself in such a way as to
produce a convergence. Such convergence ultimately
means increasing personalization—a differentiation in
heightened consciousness and freedom.

The projection of the lines of evolutionary movement
toward the unification of humanity in a complex personalizing web is not, for Teilhard, simply an analogy, pointing
to the similarity between what is happening at the world
level and what happened as self-consciousness developed
in individual man. He is not just speaking metaphorically.
Just as convergence at the individual level brought actual
conscious centers into being, so convergence at the social
and cultural level culminates in an actual personal and
personalizing center of consciousness. The end point of the
process Teilhard calls "Omega."

"Evolution is an ascent towards consciousness. . . . Therefore it should culminate forwards in some sort of supreme
consciousness."[16] We are, he thinks, actually experiencing

"the first symptoms of . . . the birth of some single centre
from the convergent beams of millions of elementary centres dispersed over the surface of the thinking earth." And
since union differentiates,

> By its structure Omega, in its ultimate principle, can only
> be a distinct Centre radiating at the core of a system of centres;
> a grouping in which personalization of the All and personaliza-
> tions of the elements reach their maximum, simultaneously and
> without merging, under the influence of a supremely autono-
> mous focus of union.[17]

But a synthesis of centers can be achieved only if contact is made "centre to centre . . . and *not otherwise,*" and
such a relationship can only be called love.[18]

> Love alone is capable of uniting living beings in such a way
> as to complete and fulfil them, for it alone takes them and joins
> them by what is deepest in themselves.[19]

For Teilhard, love is not peculiar to man. It is not only a
property of all of life, in a variety of forms, but it is not
lacking anywhere as the "internal propensity to unite"
even at the most rudimentary level. If it were not present
as such a propensity even at the level of the molecule, it
could never appear at the human level.[20] Teilhard accepts
the "possibility, indeed the reality, of some source of love
and object of love at the summit of the world."[21] The
radiation of this love is not simply the end point of the
process of convergence. The Omega point is not simply
future; it is a present reality. Teilhard believes he must
assume the present reality and power of the Omega in
order to explain the reality of the love that does exist, for
"love dies in contact with the impersonal and the anonymous."

For love to be possible there must be co-existence. Accordingly, however marvellous its foreseen figure, Omega could never even so much as equilibrate the play of human attractions and repulsions if it did not act with equal force, that is to say with the same stuff of proximity.[22]

Furthermore, "to satisfy the ultimate requirements of our action, Omega must be independent of the collapse of the forces with which evolution is woven."[23] In other words, man's realization of the perishable nature of all that touches his life and the evolutionary process itself would undercut the very ground for action, if it were not for some guarantee of irreversibility and transcendence. Courage to be, finally, demands the assumption of or the awareness of the present imperishable reality of Omega.

Moreover, Teilhard believes that the very postulate of an Omega point could not be reached from a study of the phenomenon of evolution were Omega only a remote and ideal focus destined to emerge in some distant future. One would see "no other energy of a personal nature . . . save that represented by the sum of human persons."[24] If, however, Omega is "already in existence and operative," there ought to be some traces of its influence. At the lower stages of evolution it could, of course, show its effects only in an impersonal way under the "veil of biology"; but with the emergence of persons, one would expect to see some excess of "personal, extra-human energy."[25]

III. CHRISTIANITY AND EVOLUTION

In an epilogue to *The Phenomenon of Man*, Teilhard, still trying to maintain the phenomenological perspective as he conceives it, looks for such evidence. He finds it in what he calls "the Christian Phenomenon." The Christian fact stands before us, and for Teilhard even at the level of observation, apart from religious conviction, it points to the operative presence of the postulated Omega point. First of all, the Christian phenomenon, in its creed and in the life it has promoted, "fits" the phenomenological reading of evolutionary process. Its theology, with its personalism and universalism, parallels what is demanded by the direction of evolution. Its cosmic dimension, sometimes lost or overlooked in certain forms of Christian thought, duplicates the perspective demanded by evolutionary thought. The Kingdom of God is not just "a big family"; "it is a prodigious biological operation—that of the Redeeming Incarnation."[26] This is the meaning of the teaching of Paul and John about Christ, a teaching which emphasizes the cosmic dimensions of Christ's presence and action. For them, "to create, to fulfil and to purify the world is, for God, to unify it by uniting it organically with himself."

How does he unify it? By partially immersing himself in things, by becoming "element," and then, from this point of vantage in the heart of matter, assuming control and leadership of what we *now* call evolution.[27]

When Paul speaks of God's being all in all, it is just this culmination that he points to—God becomes the Center of centers. Says Teilhard:

And so exactly, so perfectly does this coincide with the Omega Point that doubtless I should never have ventured to envisage the latter or formulate the hypothesis rationally if, in my consciousness as a believer, I had not found not only its speculative model but also its living reality.[28]

But the parallel between Christian thinking and the projected implications of evolution goes beyond thought.

Christianity embodies itself in the lives of men as well as in their thinking. It has brought into being a "specifically new state of consciousness"—Christian love. Whether founded on illusion or not, Christian love and its results are part of the Christian phenomenon. The mystics and thousands of ordinary men and women have incarnated this love in their lives. This genuinely universal love has not only been conceived and preached; it has been "shown to be psychologically possible and operative in practice."[29]

Finally, what Christianity preaches and demands and what evolutionary process seems to indicate about the meaning of man's life and his fulfillment implies a power of growth for Christianity and the possibility of coincidence and mutual enrichment of Christian and evolutionary thinking which means new vitality for Christianity even as the other ancient religions are in crisis because of their incompatibility with the new world of scientific thought.

Though frightened for a moment by evolution, the Christian now perceives that what it offers him is nothing but a magnificent means of feeling more at one with God and of giving himself more to him. . . . And it is in no way metaphorical to say that man finds himself capable of experiencing and discovering his God in the whole length, breadth and depth of the world in movement. To be able to say literally to God that one loves him, not only with all one's body, all one's heart and all one's soul, but with every fibre of the unifying universe— that is a prayer that can only be made in space-time.[80]

IV. BEYOND APPEARANCES

Not all Teilhard's thinking and writing stays at the level of phenomena and their implications. Up to this point in the development of his thought Teilhard insists that he is not dealing with ultimate causes or final interpretations, with philosophical or theological issues in their own right. He says again and again that what he has been looking for and what he has found is "the experimental law of recurrence." His interest, however, has been at the macro-phenomenal level, that is, he wants the synthetic vision—the whole phenomenon of man that reaches back to the development of the cosmos and of life and is to be read forward on the basis of the present and the past. Even his view of the ultimate outcome and his conviction that the universe as a whole has direction, which are in "a strict sense, undemonstrable to science," seem to him to arise out of the phenomenological perspective and stay within that sphere.

It is clear that, although Teilhard wishes in much of his writing to keep clear of any transphenomenological per-spective both to win fellow scientists to his point of view and to avoid theological conflict with the church, at other times he looks at the same facts from a Christian perspec-tive. He explicitly holds that there need be no conflict between these perspectives and that they will enrich and support each other.

From a clear Christian perspective Teilhard writes out of a mystic's vision and experience:

Throughout my life, through my life, the world has little by little caught fire in my sight until, aflame all around me, it has become almost completely luminous from within. . . . Such has been my experience in contact with the earth—the diaphany of the divine at the heart of the universe on fire. . . . Christ; His heart; a fire: capable of penetrating everywhere and, gradually, spreading everywhere.[31]

God really is everywhere and in all things."God is as out-stretched and tangible as the atmosphere in which we are bathed."[32] Only one thing prevents us from responding to him—our inability to see him. Teilhard sees his own task as teaching men "how to see God everywhere, to see Him in all that is most hidden, most solid and most ultimate in the world."[33]

It is obvious for one whose vision of God is so deeply related to his vision of nature and the world, and who also has so vividly interpreted the evolutionary vision of nature and the world that the two must come together. The world is one world; everything forms a single whole, and within the whole everything is linked to everything else. We live in the midst of a network of cosmic influences, and "in each one of us, through matter, the whole history of the world is . . . reflected."[34] In and through this network of cosmic influences, Teilhard sees the power of the incarnate Word penetrating matter itself. The incarnation is not in this sense once and for all; it is an ongoing dynamic process which will be "complete only when the part of chosen substance contained in every object . . . has rejoined the final Centre of its completion."[35] And man collaborates in this process of incarnation: "With each one of our *works*, we labour—atomically, but no less really—to build the Pleroma; that is to say, we bring to Christ a little fulfil-ment."[36] God, then, is not withdrawn from the tangible sphere. "He is waiting for us at every moment in our ac-tion, in our work of the moment."[37] Thus, "for those who know how to see," nothing earthly is profane. Even our passivities—those of growth and those of diminishment (Teilhard means the destructive forces that press upon us) are capable of entering into this process. They can be transfigured. God can be found even "in and through every death," for these passivities of diminishment can become the means of deliverance from self-centeredness. In words of prayer Teilhard writes, "O God, grant that I may understand that it is You . . . who are painfully parting the fibres of my being in order to penetrate to the very marrow of my substance and bear me away within Yourself."[38]

Again, "Jesus on the Cross is both the symbol and the reality of the immense labour of the centuries which has, little by little, raised up the created spirit and brought it back to the depths of the divine context."[39] Little by little, says Teilhard, the work is being done. "Thanks to the multitude of individuals and vocations, the Spirit of God insinuates itself everywhere and is everywhere at work."[40]

This presence of God in and through all things, creating and redeeming, moving the evolutionary processes toward consummation, is what constitutes the milieu of human life, a *divine* milieu. "By means of all created things, without exception, the divine assails us, penetrates us and moulds us."[41] "Incomparably near and tangible—for it presses in upon us through all the forces of the universe—it nevertheless eludes our grasp so constantly that we can never seize it here below except by raising ourselves, uplifted on its waves, to the extreme limit of our efforts."[42] And yet, however vast this divine milieu is, it is a center drawing all together into unity.

The essence of Christianity consists in asking the question: "What is . . . the concrete link which binds all these universal entities together and confers on them a final power of gaining hold of us?" and in answering: "The Word Incarnate, Our Lord Jesus Christ." God is present to us not only by enfolding and penetrating us, by creating and preserving us; he also gives us the gift of participated being—under the form of an essential aspiration toward him. And he molds us for that supreme and complex reality, the mysterious Pleroma, which Teilhard calls "the quantitative repletion and qualitative consummation of all things."[43] It is through the "network of the organizing forces of the total Christ" that "God exerts pressure, in us and upon us."[44] Teilhard calls this "the omnipresence of christification." All of this is not simply Teilhard's interpretation of Pauline and Johannine thought about the cosmic Christ and the incarnation. It is also his view of the meaning of the Mass.

When the priest says, *Hoc est Corpus meum,* transforming the bread, this Sacramental operation does not end with that local and momentary event. In reality there is only one Mass and one communion. All communions everywhere are one communion. The incarnation is a single event that has been developing in the world. The Eucharistic influence upon our human natures extends its energy necessarily, because of the effects of the interweaving of all that is, into the "less luminous regions that sustain us." "At every moment the Eucharistic Christ controls . . . the whole movement of the universe," at least as understood from the point of view of the organization of the Pleroma.[45]

For Teilhard, such an understanding is another way of coming at the meaning of the divine milieu, now seen as being defined by the "extensions" of the Eucharist. In Christ we live and move and have our being. One should speak, he says, not so much of the appearance of God in the universe as of his *transparence* in the universe. The divine milieu discloses itself as the "incandescence of the inward layers of being," and such disclosure is a gift. We can only pray for it. Thus Teilhard, as a Christian, has a new perspective on man and his journey, a perspective not in conflict with that which emerges from the evolutionary vision, but one which discloses a deeper meaning in that vision.

Across the immensity of time and the disconcerting multiplicity of individuals, one single operation is taking place: the annexation to Christ of His chosen; one single thing is being made: the Mystical Body of Christ, starting from all the sketchy spiritual powers scattered throughout the world.[46]

And the end, the Parousia, is a vision of Christ as "All-in-everything; of the universe moved and compenetrated by God in the totality of its evolution."[47] "To desire the Parousia, all we have to do is to let the very heart of the earth, as we Christianise it, beat within us."[48] To this vocation man is called. This is his dignity, his meaning, and his fulfillment.

4: *Karl Marx —*
Economic Man

KARL MARX, one of the most influential thinkers of the last century, was born May 5, 1818. He studied law at Bonn and Berlin and then went on to be an editor, writer, and founder of the modern Communist movement. Settling first in Paris, then in Brussels, from which he was expelled, he was banished from Germany and in 1849 moved to London. In England he became a serious student of economics and wrote there his major work, *Das Kapital.* Marx was the intellectual leader of what came to be known as "scientific socialism," and he is looked upon as the ideological founder of international Communism.

For many today the name of Marx is a kind of red flag because of his association with contemporary Communism. This makes it all the more important for us to understand what he himself said about man and what the ground for his appeal has been. We must be especially careful, however, about identifying Marx at every point with what goes under the name of Marxism, just as we should be careful about identifying Christ with all that has called itself Christian through the centuries. Furthermore, there are differing interpretations of what Marx "really taught." The following account is an attempted synthesis using both Marx's early writings and his later ones. It presupposes the view that Marx's essential vision remained constant while his manner of communicating this vision and his vocabulary changed from the earlier to the later period.

I. WHAT IS WRONG WITH MAN
ACCORDING TO KARL MARX?

Marx's fundamental conviction about man is that he is not fully human. He is an alienated dehumanized being. In fact, the whole history of man is a history of his increasing alienation and dehumanization. The term alienation points to an internal split in man and to the separation of man from others. It refers to his somehow having become foreign to himself, to his activities, to his fellowmen. His inward unity is broken; his sense of his own activity and perception of others is as of something foreign and apart. While the phenomenon of alienation colors all of life for Marx, its decisive focus is in the economic sphere.

What man is at any given time in history is decisively affected by the forms of economic life that obtain, according to Marx. Moreover, man's life changes and can be changed with an alteration of the mode of economic production. In his *The Condition of the Working Man in England in 1844,* Engels (Marx's collaborator) gives a dramatic illustration of both these points. He describes the condition of the weavers in the days of handicraft. The workers

vegetated throughout a passably comfortable existence, leading a righteous and peaceful life in all piety and probity. . . . They did no more than they chose to do, and yet they earned what they needed. They had leisure for healthful work in garden and field, work which in itself was recreation, and they could take part besides in the recreations and games of their neighbors, and all these games . . . contributed to their physical health and vigor.

Then came new inventions and factories. The laborers were now herded together in the great factory towns. Engels quotes Carlyle's *Chartism* to show the change. Now,

their trade is of the nature of gambling; they live by it like gamblers. . . . Black, mutinous discontent devours them; simply the miserablest feeling that can inhabit the heart of man. English commerce . . . makes all paths uncertain for them, all life a bewilderment; society, steadfastness, peaceable continuance, the first blessing of man, are not theirs. . . . This world is for them no home, but a dingy prison-house, of reckless unthrift, rebellion, rancour, indignation against themselves and against all men.[1]

Marx and Engels have often been understood to mean that nothing but the economic factor is determinative, but this seems to be untrue. Other factors interact (political, juridical, religious, etc.), but economic necessity always ultimately asserts itself.[2]

II. THE THREE FORMS OF ALIENATION

For Marx the core of the process of alienation is to be found in the process of production. "As individuals express their life, so they are. What they are, therefore, coincides with their production, both with what they produce and how they produce. The nature of individuals thus depends on the material conditions of this production."[3] Man's very work becomes the source of his alienation, of his inward division of himself from himself.

A. *Alienation from Self*

This is seen in man's alienation from the product of his labor. Under present and historical conditions of work, the object produced by man's labor—the product, in other words—"now confronts him in the shape of an alien thing, a power independent of the producer."[4] In this view, Marx depends on what he takes to be the character of the wage system and his theory of surplus value.[5]

The product that the worker makes is, for Marx, an objectification of his work, and yet through the wage system he loses something of himself in producing it, since he does not keep the whole value of that which he has produced. The product of his labor is that which is returned in wages. Moreover, what he has created but does not retain becomes set over against him, as a power over him, and is used against him by those who have claimed it. The result of this process is:

> The worker becomes poorer, the more wealth he produces and the more his production increases in power and extent.
> All these consequences follow from the fact that the worker is related to the product of his labor as an alien object. For it is clear on this presupposition that the more the worker expends himself in work, the more powerful becomes the world of objects which he creates in face of himself, the poorer he becomes in his inner life and the less he belongs to himself. . . . The worker puts his life into the object and his life then belongs no longer to himself but to the object. The greater his activity, therefore, the less he possesses. . . . The alienation of the worker in his product means not only that his labor becomes an object, assumes an external existence, but that it exists independently outside himself, that it stands opposed to him as an autonomous power. The life which he has given to the object sets itself against him as an alien and hostile force.[6]

B. *Alienation from the Work Process*

Not only, says Marx, is man's labor alienated in the product of his labor, but in the process of producing it he no longer feels that he himself is "in" his work. His working is something somehow foreign to him. This change could be illustrated by Engels' remarks about the weavers. Marx himself expresses his judgment about what happens to the worker and the work processes in capitalism:

They mutilate the laborer into a fragment of a man, degrade him to the level of an appendage of a machine, destroy every remnant of charm in his work and turn it into hated toil; they estrange from him the intellectual potentialities of the labor process.[7]

Thus the social relations of production become a form of bondage and servitude. Labor is no longer self-activity engaged in for its joy and in spontaneity. It becomes a form of evolutionary servitude. Marx writes, in answer to the question, What constitutes the alienation of labor:

First . . . the work is external to the worker, that it is not part of his nature, and that consequently he does not fulfill himself in his work, but denies himself, has a feeling of misery rather than well being, does not develop freely his mental and physical energies but is physically exhausted and mentally debased. The worker therefore feels himself at home only during his leisure time, whereas at work he feels homeless. His work is not voluntary but imposed, forced labor. It is not the satisfaction of a need, but only the means for satisfying other needs. Its alien character is clearly shown by the fact that as soon as there is no physical or other compulsion it is avoided like the plague. External labor, labor in which man alienates himself, is a labor of self-sacrifice, of mortification. Finally, the external character of work for the worker is shown by the fact that it is not his own work but work for someone else, that in work he does not belong to himself but to another person.[8]

C. Alienation from Other Men

The result of these forms of alienation is alienation from other men. The unity of life with life is broken, and man is pitted against man. One way to talk about how this happens and what it means is to speak of the class struggle. Another way is to say simply not only that groups of men are in conflict with each other but that man *exploits* and is *exploited* by his fellowmen. Man *uses* man and is used by him. The result is something less than the fully human life. It is *dehumanization*. It will be worth our effort to note certain aspects of this process of dehumanization as Marx observed it.

1. *Man is turned into a commodity.* For Marx, the historic forms of the economic means of production and exchange treat man as a commodity to be utilized. He is just another object, like coal or iron ore, valued primarily in terms of his usefulness in the productive process. Marx writes:

Hence it is self-evident that the laborer is nothing else his whole life through, than labor-power, that therefore all his disposable time is by nature and law labor time, to be devoted to the self-expansion of capital. . . . It usurps the time for the growth, development, and maintenance of the body. It steals the time required for the consumption of fresh air and sunlight. It higgles over a meal time, incorporating it where possible with the process of production itself, so that food is given to the laborer as to a mere means of production, as coal is supplied to the boiler, grease and oil to the machinery. It reduces the sound sleep needed for the restoration, reparation, refreshment of the bodily powers to just so many hours of torpor as the revival of an organism, absolutely exhausted, renders essential. It is not the normal maintenance of the labor-power, no matter how diseased, compulsory, and painful it may be, which is to determine the limits of the laborer's period of repose. Capital cares nothing for the length of life of labor power. All that concerns it is simply and solely the maximum of labor power that can be rendered fluent in a working day. It attains this end by shortening the extent of the laborer's life, as a greedy farmer snatches increased produce from the soil by robbing it of its fertility.[9]

2. *Man is mistreated.* Under capitalistic modes of economic organization, as Marx saw it, anything goes. Little children can be put into the sweatshops. Men can be made to work under inhuman conditions in mines with no concern shown for their health or dangers to life. Women can be crowded into narrow and unsanitary rooms in the midst of dangerous machinery, with no thought for their being more than disposable elements in the productive process.

Marx made much of the reports provided in his day by the English factory inspectors. Reporting on child labor under nineteenth-century conditions, he wrote:

William Wood, nine years old, was seven years and ten months when he began to work. He ran moulds (carried ready-moulded articles into the drying room), afterwards bringing back the empty mould from the beginning. He came to work every day in the week at 6 a.m. and left about 9 p.m. "I work till nine o'clock at night, six days in the week. I have done so for seven or eight weeks." Fifteen hours of labour for child of seven years old! . . . G. Apsten: "That boy of nine . . . when he was seven years old I used to carry him on my back to and fro through the snow, and he used to have sixteen hours a day. . . . I have often knelt down to feed him as he stood by the machine, for he could not leave it or stop." . . . For all these, children and adults alike . . . the average work for the eighteen months has been at the very last seven days, five hours, or seventy-eight and one-half hours a week. For the six weeks ending May 2nd this year the average was higher—eight days or eighty-four hours a week.[10]

Commenting on the dangers of capitalist production he declared:

According to the report on Coal Mines Accidents (February 6, 1862), a total of 8,466 were killed in the ten years 1852–61. But the report admits that this number is far too low, because in the first few years, when the inspectors had just been installed and their districts were far too large, a great many accidents and deaths were not reported. The very fact that the number of accidents, though still very high, has decreased markedly since the inspection system was established, and this in spite of the limited powers and insufficient numbers of the inspectors, demonstrates the natural tendency of capitalist exploitation. These human sacrifices are mostly due to the inordinate avarice of the mine owners. Very often they had only one shaft sunk, so that apart from the lack of effective ventilation there was no escape were this shaft to become obstructed.[11]

Marx felt that the evidence showed that capitalist production considered labor expendable. When human beings were no longer usable in the productive process, they were junked. Capitalist production, according to Marx, is a process of self-aggrandizement of capital. It aims to get the greatest surplus value from the living labor power, which it consumes in the process.

√ 3. *Man's worst appetites are encouraged.* As if it were not enough to treat man as a commodity and to be careless of his health and life in his conditions of work, the system panders to the worst side of man's being. Marx writes:

The expansion of production and of needs becomes an ingenious and always calculating subservience to inhuman, depraved, unnatural, and imaginary appetites. Private property does not know how to change crude need into *human* need; its idealism is fantasy, caprice, and fancy. No eunuch flatters his tyrant more shamefully or seeks by more infamous means to stimulate his jaded appetite, in order to gain some favor, than does the eunuch of industry, the entrepreneur, in order to acquire a few silver coins or to charm the gold from the purse of his dearly beloved neighbor. Every product is a bait by means of which the individual tries to entice the essence of the other person, his money. Every real or potential need is a weakness which will draw the bird into the lime. Universal exploitation of human communal life. As every imperfection of man is a bond with heaven, a point at which his heart is accessible to the priest, so every want is an opportunity for approaching one's neighbor with an air of friendship, and saying, "Dear friend, I will give you what you need, but you know the *condition sine qua non.* You know what ink you must use in signing yourself over to me. I shall swindle you while providing your enjoyment. The entrepreneur accedes to the most depraved fancies of his neighbor, plays the role of pander between him and his needs, awakens unhealthy appetites in him, and watches for every weakness in order, later, to claim the remuneration for this labor of love.[12]

III. The Sources of Alienation

Among students of the early Marx, there is some disagreement about the original sources of alienation. But wherever and however alienation began, it is clear that Marx believed that money and the drive for self-aggrandizement were intimately related to it. "Money" he calls "the alienated essence of man's work and his being." This alien being rules over him, and "he worships it. . . ."[13] In another place he writes:

Money is regarded as an omnipotent being. . . . Money is the *pander* between need and object, between human life and the means of subsistence. But that which mediates my life mediates also the existence of other men for me. It is for me the *other* person.[14]

Commenting on Shakespeare's description of the function of money in his play *Timon of Athens,* Marx writes of how the individual becomes what his money can buy, and others become for him what their money makes possible. We are not ourselves—we are what our money is and what our money makes us. Money is the alienated and self-alienating power of humanity.

Money appears, then, as a disruptive power for the individual and for the bonds of society. It changes fidelity into infidelity, love into hate, hate into love, virtue into vice and vice into virtue. It makes stupidity appear to be intelligence and intelligence stupidity.[15]

Money is seen by Marx as one of the keys to the self-alienating process. Men are not what they really are, and their relations to others are not products of their own integrity, but of what the passion for money and the power of money makes of them.

In his later writing Marx appears to think of alienation as primarily derivable from the division of labor and the consequent origin of private property, and this view of things was not lacking in his early writings as well. When a division between physical and mental labor arose it became possible for some to live off the surplus labor of others and to accumulate this surplus in the form of capital. This was the beginning of private property apart from personal property. One group was thus divided against another. A hostile social relation of man to man and of class to class were the outcome of this phenomenon.

What is the end result of this process? Marx answers:

Accumulation of wealth at one pole is, therefore, at the same time accumulation of misery, agony of toil, slavery, ignorance, brutality, mental degradation at the opposite pole, i.e., on the side of the class that produces its own product in the form of capital.[16]

When this happens, and it is part of the necessity of the historical process that it should happen, then the despotism of capital will have become unbearable. The workers of the world will unite and throw off their chains. There will be a world revolution in which private property is abolished or expropriated. The abolition of private property through such a revolution will bring, according to Marx, a radical reversal in the condition of man. Alienation will be overcome. Man will really appropriate human nature. It will be the "definitive resolution of the antagonism between man and nature and between man and man."[17]

IV. The Ultimate Outcome—A New Kind of Man and a New Social Order

In his early formulation of the vision of the new world acoming, Marx foresaw the recovery of human freedom. Man would be released to a new nonacquisitive life. He would enjoy his productive activity. Many of his potentialities which had been thwarted would now develop spontaneously. He writes:

The supersession of private property is therefore the complete emancipation of all the human qualities and senses. It is this emancipation because these qualities and senses have become *human,* from the subjective as well as the objective point of view.

This is to be seen as a reversal of man's situation in which

private property has made us so stupid and partial that an object is only *ours* when we have it, when it exists for us as capital or when it is directly eaten, drunk, worn, inhabited, etc., in short utilized in some way.[18]

The new man not only has new potentialities released. He is independent.

A being does not regard himself as independent unless he is his own master, and he is only his own master when he owes his existence to himself. A man who lives by the favor of another considers himself a dependent being.[19]

But the realm of freedom does not commence until the point is passed where labor under the compulsion of necessity and external utility is required. Since material production is necessary for existence itself,

freedom in this field can only consist in socialized man, the associated producers, rationally regulating their interchange with Nature, bringing it under their common control, instead of being ruled by it as by the blind forces of Nature, and achieving this with the least expenditure of energy and under conditions most favourable to, and worthy of, their human nature.[20]

That Marx's vision, spelled out in his early writings, was focal to the most important single document of Marxism is seen at the end of the second section of the *Communist Manifesto:*

When in the course of development, class distinctions have disappeared, and all production has been concentrated in the hands of a vast association of the whole nation, the public power will lose its political character. . . . In place of the old bourgeois society, with its classes and class antagonisms, we shall have an association in which the free development of each is the condition for the free development of all.[21]

This vision of the new man and the new society remained one of the chief attractions of the Communist movement.

The Programme of the Communist International adopted at the Sixth Congress contains the following prediction:

Communist society will abolish the class division of society, i.e., simultaneously with the abolition of anarchy in production, it will abolish all forms of exploitation and oppression of man by man. Society will no longer consist of antagonistic classes in conflict with each other, but will present a united common-wealth of labour. For the first time in its history mankind will take its fate into its own hands. Instead of destroying innumerable human lives and incalculable wealth in struggles between classes and nations, mankind will devote all its energy to the struggle against the forces of nature, to the developing and strengthening of its own collective might. . . .

The abolition of private property and the disappearance of classes will do away with the exploitation of man by man. Work will cease to be toiling for the benefit of a class enemy; instead of being merely a means of livelihood it will become a necessity of life: want and economic inequality, the misery of enslaved classes, and a wretched standard of life generally will disappear; the hierarchy created in the division of the labour system will be abolished, together with the antagonism between mental and manual labour; and the last vestige of the social inequality of the sexes will be removed. At the same time, the organs of class domination, and the State in the first place, will disappear also.[22]

5: *Sigmund Freud —*
Psychological Man

LIKE MARX, Freud, the founder of psychoanalysis, was one of the great figures who helped to change the interpretation of man in the twentieth century. He was born in 1856 in Moravia, lived in Vienna between his fourth and eighty-second year, and was finally forced to flee to London in 1938 by the Nazi annexation of Austria. He died there in 1939. As a young man Freud turned to the study of physiology and medicine. He was interested in research, but since financial circumstances made such a career difficult, he began his career as a practicing neurologist. However, he says in his autobiography: "Anyone who wanted to make a living from the treatment of nervous patients must clearly be able to do something to help them. My therapeutic arsenal contained only two weapons, electrotherapy and hypnotism."[1] He soon found that the electrotherapy was useless and he went on, as a result of his studies with Jean Charcot in Paris, to explore the psychological roots of hysteria. This work led him into association with a distinguished Viennese physician, Dr. Josef Breuer. This early collaboration became the seedbed for many of the ideas that led to the development of psychoanalysis. Freud wrote many works during his lifetime; the one he himself regarded as his greatest book was *The Interpretation of Dreams* (1900). Though he encountered a good deal of initial resistance to his new ideas, many of these same ideas have become common coin among those who may know nothing of their source. Over the years his views have been attacked and alternative schools of psychoanalytic thought have arisen; but Freud still remains the master and the seminal mind. His influence has gone far beyond the limited circle of psychology and psychiatry into the fields of literature, art, and anthropology. In the following discussion we shall avoid the technicalities of Freud's language and analysis wherever possible. The reader should recognize, however, that this is possible in only a limited way, for Freud had to devise a new language to describe and account for many of the things he believed he had discovered about man.

I. What Is Going on Inside Man?

Trained as a physician, Freud's interest in neurology led him to concentrate on the treatment of nervous disorders. In the course of his work with his patients, he made discoveries about human behavior and devised theories to explain what he had discovered that were to shock his world and change the course of medical treatment of the "mentally ill."

A. *Man's behavior is determined by psychological processes of which he is unaware—the unconscious.*

From his early work with the Viennese physician Breuer, Freud became convinced that human behavior and thinking are strongly influenced, even determined, both by past experiences and by present internal forces of which people are unaware. He saw in men "unconscious processes" at work over which they had no control and of which they had no knowledge.

An illustration from the earliest work of Breuer will both show the way in which this discovery was made and clarify its meaning. Breuer had been treating a twenty-one-year-old girl who for a number of months had been very disturbed. Among her symptoms were paralysis of the arms, hallucinations, alterations of sight and speech. For no apparent reason she had great difficulty in taking a drink. She would take a glass of water in her hand, but as it touched her lips she would push it away again, unable to drink it. Under hypnosis she disclosed that she had once entered her room to find a disgusting little dog (which belonged to her English governess, whom she also disliked) drinking out of a glass. She said nothing because she wanted to be polite. In the course of this disclosure Breuer recounts, "she gave energetic expression to her strangulated anger." She then asked for a drink, "and without any inhibition drank a great deal of water, awaking from the hypnosis with the glass at her lips."[2] With this the disturbance disappeared.

Breuer continues, describing his further discussions with the patient: "Every single symptom of this complicated, morbid picture was separately taken up, and the various occasions during which it appeared were related in reverse order, beginning with the days before the patient became bedridden, and backward to the time of its first appearance. When this was related, the symptom was thereby permanently removed."[3]

Freud later found other methods of probing the causes and relieving the difficulties of his patients (free association and dream interpretation). The basic insight that such symptoms have definite causes in earlier experience, and that these determinative experiences are not known to or remembered by the patient in his conscious awareness, was confirmed again.

B. *Even trivial and apparently meaningless behavior has a cause and a meaning.*

Further confirmation of the operation of unconscious processes in the lives of all men was given by Freud in his investigations of the psychopathology of everyday life. Slips of the tongue or pen, misreading and mishearing, forgetting names and the like, were seen as traceable to similar roots. They are not accidental. Dreams too bring us particularly close to the phenomena of the unconscious dimension of human life. Freud came to understand dreams as the reflection of this depth of our lives of which we are ordinarily unaware.

C. *Why are some processes unconscious?*

Why is an individual ordinarily unable to be aware of these influences which affect this thought, feeling, and behavior? What blocks awareness? What blots out the memory of certain experiences whose power yet continues to govern one's life? Freud's answer was *repression.* Repression is the process by which painful, threatening, or unduly disturbing experiences are rendered inaccessible to conscious awareness. They are blocked from awareness but not from continuing influence.

Freud's efforts to penetrate the processes of repression and of *resistance* to readmitting repressed material to awareness led him to develop an extensive theory of the inner life of man and of man's development through childhood. His studies led him to interpret the process of repression in the light of his understanding of man's inner conflict.

D. *Man's inner life is a battleground of contending forces.*

What man feels, thinks, and does is in the reflection of the conflict going on inside him. The individual has rela-

tively little control over the outcome of this conflict, since
it involves forces of which he is not consciously aware. In
the course of his lifetime Freud describes this conflict in
a variety of ways. He sees it, for example, as a conflict between what he calls the pleasure principle and the reality
principle.

Man is seen by Freud as a creature of desire (instinct
or drive). Human energy is directed toward pleasure and
away from pain (this is the pleasure principle). But the
world is not such that a free pursuit of pleasure (the
gratification of desire) is possible. Reality frustrates this
unrestricted pursuit. Pleasure must be renounced for the
sake of life in society (this pressure of reality upon the
individual Freud calls the reality principle). Under certain conditions this conflict produces mental illness and
under all conditions such conflict lies behind the fact of
repression.

Freud tries to spell out more specifically the nature of
this conflict between the pleasure principle and the reality
principle in his account of the inner life of the individual.
He sees the psychic life of the individual constituted by
the interaction of three processes, which he calls the _id_,
the _ego_, and the _superego_. The id aspect of personality is
entirely unconscious (outside conscious awareness). It is
the source of the psychic energy of the individual and is
entirely governed by the pleasure principle. The ego derives its energy from the id. It is partly conscious and
partly unconscious. It is the "executive," the coordinator
which, governed by the reality principle, relates the individual to the demands of the real world. The superego
is constituted by the inherited social standards and the
moral values of the parents. It is the critic, the conscience,
which tries to compel the ego to repress the unacceptable
pressures of the id. The struggle within man can be now

described as a struggle between the id, the ego, and the
superego. The id might be said to be the factor of desire;
the ego, that of reason; the superego, that of morality.

E. *The child is important.*

Freud's view of man and of inner conflict is further complicated because he takes the fact of development seriously. The child is seen as passing through a series of
chronologically ordered stages of development. The importance of understanding the individual from the devel-
opmental point of view lies in the fact that each individual
carries his past with him. At each stage he faces the
handling of the id-ego-superego struggle under different
conditions. His resolution of the struggle or his way of
handling it at a given period of his development is carried
with him into the following stages. His way of meeting
life is thus being laid down. He carries forward both his
resolved conflicts and his unresolved conflicts.

F. *Sexuality is important.*

From his experience in working with patients Freud
early became convinced that their difficulties in living
were closely connected with the damming up of their
sexual energies. He saw the sexual instinct, along with the
instinct for self-preservation, as one of the two great driving instincts in human life. "Sexual" had a rather narrow
meaning for Freud at this time. As time went on, the notion of sexuality was broadened. The term "sexual" came
to denote any pleasurable body sensations and in addition
the feelings associated with the deflection of such energies
into various socially acceptable substitute activities.

The important fact to note at this point is that Freud
came to see the child as having a sexual life. The develop-
mental process ordered into sequential stages is seen as

determined by the localization of energy and pleasure in one or another part of the body. The earliest stage—the oral—is that in which satisfactions are obtained chiefly through the mouth, in nursing and thumb-sucking, and later in biting and chewing. The second—the anal—centers satisfaction around the elimination processes. The third—the phallic—comes into its own when the child discovers the possibilities of pleasure through his genitals. There follows the latency period, and then in adolescence there is a reactivation of the earlier impulses and the opening up of the possibility of a more mature genital stage.

According to Freud, an individual experiencing that kind of difficulty later in life which we call neurosis is one who has failed to handle successfully the inner conflict between id-ego-superego at one of these earlier sexually defined stages. Either he has carried forward into later life an inadequate resolution of his earlier struggle, or under pressure he has reverted to or regressed to an earlier solution that is not adequate to adult life.

Freud saw one of the central failures in what he called the Oedipal situation. This is the situation that marks the phallic period of the child's life. At this point, Freud thought, the child is sexually attracted to the parent of the opposite sex and becomes hostile toward the parent of the same sex. This situation creates fear, since the child recognizes the unacceptability of his feelings. This is an example of the opposition between the pleasure and the reality principles.

G. *Anxiety is the driving power in neurosis and in repression.*

The threatening character of the Oedipal situation, the possibility of punishment—of the loss of love, loss of the

penis (castration fear), and later the loss of the approval
of society and the fear of ostracism—is experienced in
anxiety. In order to overcome the threat and quiet the
anxiety, the individual *represses* his sexual desires. Neurosis occurs when repression takes place but is not finally
successful. The repressed returns in a disguised form and
reactivates the anxiety, which then must be handled
through a variety of defenses.

Inner conflict, producing anxiety, is thus the mark of
the inner life of every man. Id forces are constantly welling
up from below. Superego forces are constantly exerting
pressure from above. The ego must handle these forces in
the face of the demands of reality. When the ego is relatively weak (as in childhood) and the anxiety created is
especially powerful, the conflict may be unsuccessfully
resolved, resulting in neurosis.

Repression is, of course, the major way the organism
handles such an anxiety-creating situation. It blocks from
awareness, pushes back into unconsciousness, the feelings
that well up from the id region. But there are additional
methods which may be resorted to. Some of these may be
mentioned. The individual may resort to a kind of inver-
sion of what might be otherwise repressed. His sexual
interest, for example, may be transmuted into a horror of
sex—a form of prudery such as participation in the cen-
soring of pornographic materials. This is called a "reversal
formation." Or he may rationalize his behavior—substi-
tuting socially acceptable reasons for behavior or ideas
that have motivations which are not socially acceptable.
Or he may project his own unadmissable feelings and ideas
onto others, seeing in them what is really true of himself.
Another way of handling such anxiety is through regression: he may retreat to earlier forms of satisfaction. Neurosis represents a kind of bondage to the past—a con-

temporary mode of living in the light of the earlier failure to resolve the conflict situation adequately.

H. *Life Instinct vs. Death Instinct*

As the years went on, Freud's earlier vision of man torn by the inner conflict between sexual instincts and instincts for self-preservation was altered to a view of conflict between sex and aggression, and finally to an even more basic conflict—that between the life and the death instincts. New observations led him to reinterpret the nature of the basic conflict.

One of the new observations had to do with the tendency of the individual to repeat again and again the earlier and sometimes painful patterns of experience. This tendency certainly seemed to be a violation of the pleasure principle. Soldiers repeated their traumatic war experiences. Children relived their earlier painful experiences. The pattern of relating to an authority figure laid down in childhood was repeated again in the relationship of the patient to the analyst.

Freud identified what was going on in such compulsive repetitions with the general tendency observable at every level of life, a tendency to restore an earlier stage of things—to return to dead level, and finally to move toward the extinction of life itself. He came to see the goal of all life as death. The basic conflict he then saw as a conflict between Eros, or the life instinct, and the death instinct. Man struggles to control this conflict, and the threat of losing control produces anxiety.

Man, says Freud, has a deathward tendency built into both his biological and psychic existence. He wants to destroy himself and yet he also wants more life. Man handles the death instinct either by turning its direction against himself (masochism—pleasure gained from one's own suffering) or against others in aggression and destruction (sadism—pleasure realized from making others suffer). "Men," says Freud, "are not gentle friendly creatures wishing for love, who simply defend themselves if they are attacked, but . . . a powerful measure of desire for aggression has to be reckoned as a part of their instinctual endowment."[4]

II. HUMAN CULTURE: THE RENUNCIATION OF GRATIFICATION

Freud's theories about the individual, his development and inner conflict, led him to an interpretation of the broader phenomena of human life. In *Civilization and Its Discontents* (1930) he presents his view of human culture or civilization. Looking at actual human behavior to discover what the aims and purposes of mankind in fact are, Freud finds, "they seek happiness, they want to become happy and remain so."[5] Such happiness proves to be centered in the experience of pleasure and the avoidance of pain and discomfort. Men are governed by the pleasure principle, then, not only as individuals but in the wider culture.

But this program of man "is in conflict with the whole world, with the macrocosm as much as the microcosm. It simply cannot be put into execution, the whole constitution of things runs counter to it."[6] Man's striving for pleasure is threatened by suffering. The sources of suffering are three: his own body (which moves toward death and decomposition), the outer world, and his relations with his fellows. In order to minimize or avoid pain, man compromises. Some of course still strive primarily for pleasure through unbridled gratification of their impulses,

but, as Freud remarks, these people are penalized after a
short indulgence, and most men are willing to settle for
much less.

Perhaps it is enough to list the main methods Freud
sees man using to avoid or reduce pain:

1. Voluntary isolation—withdrawing from relationships
   with one's fellows reduces the suffering that comes
   from that source.

2. Activism—the attack on nature, trying to make it sub-
   mit, the approach through the scientific control of
   external reality.

3. Influencing body-mind

   a. Various forms of intoxication that both induce plea-
      sure and help man to ignore pain.

   b. Controlling impulses either through some method
      of annihilating the instincts as in Yogi or through
      sublimation—i.e., transferring the instinctual aims
      into such directions as cannot be frustrated in the
      outer world. For example, a few can channel off their
      instinctual energies in intellectual work, and such
      effort is relatively independent of the outer world.
      Other forms of work may serve such purposes too.

      Still others ways of expressing instinctual energies
      in such a fashion that some pleasure may be gained
      and some suffering reduced are art, religion, and
      neurosis. Art for Freud is an escape through illusion,
      through fantasy. It is recognized as such. Religion is
      escape through illusion that is unrecognized as such.
      Religion is really a mass delusion that decries the
      value of life and promulgates a view of the real
      world that is distorted, as is a delusion. Freud's view
      of religion, most clearly expressed in his *The Future
      of an Illusion*, is that religion is derived from the

child's feeling of helplessness and the longing it evokes for a father. For him it is patently infantile and incongruous with reality. The simple truth is that there is nothing corresponding to the needed "father," and man should learn to live without the illusion that there is such.

Neurotic illness is another way out for many. It offers at least substitute gratifications. Freud sees psychosis as a despairing attempt of man to revolt at his plight.

It is not only that there are forces within the physical organism or in nature that make man compromise his search for happiness through pleasure, but these forces are given embodiment also in human culture and civilization. Culture means, for Freud, the sum of the achievements and institutions that differentiate our lives from those of our animal forebears and serve to protect humanity against nature and to regulate the relations of human beings among themselves.

Though the origins of human culture are complex, Freud declares, "It is impossible to ignore the extent to which civilization is built upon renunciation of instinctual gratifications, the degree to which the existence of civilization presupposes the non-gratification (suppression, repression, or something else?) of powerful instinctual urgencies."[7]

One of the chief areas in which culture cuts off instinctual gratification is that of sex. The other is the area of man's aggressive instincts. Man is really a wolf. Who, asks Freud, has the courage to dispute this in the face of all the evidence in his own life and in history? "Those who love fairy tales do not like it when people speak of the innate tendencies in mankind toward aggression, destruction, and in addition, cruelty."[8] This tendency to aggression is what disturbs our relations with our neighbors. Civilized society is perpetually menaced with disintegration through this primary hostility of men toward one another.

Moreover, this aggressive instinct is ineradicable. It is an expression of the death instinct. Some, like the Communists, think that by changing the social or economic order they could eliminate such behavior. This hope, says Freud, is illusory. The aggressive instinct did not arise as the result of private property. It was present from the beginning in social life, and in individual life it is already present in the nursery.

Not only the life of the individual, but the life of culture is seen by Freud as the struggle between Eros and Death, between the instincts of life and the instincts of destruction. In the course of this struggle the gratification of instincts—sexual and aggressive—has to be restrained. But it is not only the limitation of instinctual gratification as such that thwarts pleasure and therefore happiness. Part of man's suffering derives from _the way_ in which culture restricts man.

According to Freud, this way is _guilt_. Man's aggressiveness is internalized, turned back against himself. The superego in the form of conscience "exercises the same propensity to harsh aggressiveness against the ego that the ego would like to enjoy against others."[9] A man may feel guilty, of course, in the face of _external_ authority, but his sense of guilt before _internal_ authority is even more devastating because it is inescapable. Both forms of guilt bring instinct renunciation and suffering, for the experience of guilt is painful. It is however "the price of progress in civilization."[10] And guilt need not be consciously felt by either the individual or the culture to have its effect. Unconscious sense of guilt in the individual expresses itself in an unconscious seeking for punishment. In the culture where the sense of guilt remains largely unconscious it is expressed in a "sort of uneasiness or discontent for which other motivations are sought."[11]

III. What Then Is the Goal for Man?

We have spent a good deal of time spelling out Freud's view of the collective and individual sicknesses of man, for these are the problems around which he centered his attention. But implicit in these views and in the understanding of the therapy addressed to this sickness is Freud's vision of health—of the fulfilled life. In one sense one could say that Freud has the supposedly unrepressed primitive—the one who can satisfy his instinctual demands without thwarting—as the healthy man. But it is clear that under the conditions of culture and civilization such fulfillment is impossible. At one point Freud defines the goal for man as "being able to work and to love." Both of these are implicit in his view of the fully developed genital level (in his theory of the stages of development centered around areas of sexual interest and activity) as the goal of the physiological and psychological unfolding of the individual life. Sickness is then arrested development, fixation, regression. Such a direction involves also a movement toward independence. Dependency ties with father or mother, or their surrogates, have been cut. The individual is alone, depending on his own judgment and strength.

And yet man's achievement is always more or less. It is never final. There is no final healing or salvation. There is always the conflict between instinct and culture, and be-

tween life and death. Freud's is a kind of Stoic view of life.
One should not expect or hope for too much. Philip Rieff
has called Freud's goal for man "psychological man." His
ethic is an "ethic of honesty."[12] Freud finally demands
only that the individual becomes freed to live without
illusion, facing himself and the issues of his life without
fantasy and without falsehood. This demand for honesty
does not lead to hedonism or to the unconditional release
of human energies, as some of Freud's interpreters have
suggested. Instinct is not to triumph over moral feeling,
but instinct and intelligence are to be reconciled. The
central problem of human life is that of authority. Authority is necessary, for man's natural impulses must be re-
stricted. But too much repression thwarts possibilities that
would otherwise be open to man. All that can be hoped
for is the correction of some of the imbalance between the
two main categories of the moral life—instinct and culture. Freud aims at producing the self-conscious prudent
man "whose mind has freed itself inwardly from authority"
(Rieff). Psychological man is the man without illusions
about himself or about his world. He can live by practical
experimental insight and so gain insight over his own
personality.

IV. ACHIEVING THE GOAL

How is man to get that measure of fulfillment which
may be available to him? How is he to become "psychological man"? The path is the analytic way. The Freudian
strategy is that of freeing the self from its tyrannies
through the intervention of the psychological expert, the
analyst. Therapy is the road to the good life, at least to as
much good life as a man can have. Man is not really capable of achieving the good life by himself. The therapist

must accompany the patient along the road to self-mastery. He can, through the rational interrogation of the patient's past (using the tools of free association and dream intrepretation), help the individual combine his drives and impulses in a more efficient balance. The analyst can help the individual uncover his hidden self. And to know oneself is finally to be known by another. Freud is, says Rieff, "a statesman of the inner life aiming at shrewd compromises with the human condition, not its basic transformation." The ideal is finally a negative ideal and ever-retreating goal. Man is to become sufficiently free to overcome what needs to be overcome; and the overcoming, which is the most one can ever hope to win, is a rational knowledge of the effects of the inherent dualisms upon one's own life. Freud, says Rieff, had "the tired wisdom of a universal healer for whom no disease can be wholly cured."[13]

There are, as we have observed, parallels in the situation faced by the individual and the culture. It may be, says Freud, that many systems of civilization or epochs—"possibly even the whole of humanity—have become 'neurotic' under the pressure of civilizing trends."[14] The psychoanalysis of society and the recommendation of therapeutic treatment might also be possible. Perhaps, says Freud, someone someday may "venture upon this research into the pathology of civilized communities."[15] Yet here too the struggle of life and death goes on, and the outcome is not sure. In 1930, Freud concluded his work *Civilization and Its Discontents* with these words, which may be a fitting conclusion to our brief exposition of his thought:

The fateful question of the human species seems to me to be whether and to what extent the cultural process developed in it will succeed in mastering the derangements of communal life caused by the human instinct of aggression and self-destruction. In this connection, perhaps the phase through which we are at this moment passing deserves special interest. Men have brought their powers of subduing the forces of nature to such a pitch that by using them they could now very easily exterminate one another to the last man. They know this—hence arises a great part of their current unrest, their rejection, their mood of apprehension. And now it may be expected that the other of the two "heavenly forces," eternal Eros, will put forth his strength so as to maintain himself alongside of his equally immortal adversary.[16]

6 : Søren Kierkegaard— Existential Man

SØREN KIERKEGAARD was a <u>Danish thinker</u> of the <u>nine-teenth century, one of the fathers of</u> the modern movement that is called <u>existentialism.</u> Brought up in a religious family, he rebelled against both his father and his father's faith while at the university. As the result of a good deal of reflection and a series of religious experiences, he underwent a radical reorientation, returned to the Christian faith, and became reconciled with his father. During the remainder of his life he wrote a series of penetrating works interpreting the meaning of human existence. These works, long neglected, began to have a decisive impact in Western philosophical and theological thought after the turn of the century. Their influence can be traced in the theological renaissance of our times through the thought of such men as Barth, Brunner, the Niebuhrs, Tillich, and many others. If we are to grasp what contemporary Christian thinkers are saying about man, it will be well to try to grasp the main lines of Kierkegaard's thought.

I. WHAT IS WRONG WITH MAN?

Kierkegaard believed that men had not become fully human; they had not reached full personhood. They were not, as he termed it, "individuals." To be fully human means to be an individual, a self with integrity, passion, freedom. Men do not truly *exist*. Their existence only approaches and falls more or less short of what it could be and what it ought to be.

In order to present Kierkegaard's understanding of the meaning of full or authentic human existence, we shall have to show in some detail what the various possibilities for existence were, as Kierkegaard described them; but first we must look at his characterization of what he found wrong with man.

A. *Spectators*

Many men, said Kierkegaard, are really spectators on life. They are not involved; they do not make basic decisions on which they stake the meaning of their own lives. They watch, they observe, they analyze. They are detached. The decisions that they do make are not fundamental. If they are thinkers, they may work out a fine scheme of thought—but it does not affect their own lives or behavior. They may preach, but they do not practice.

Another form of the same kind of detachment is seen in those who drift along on the surface of life, tasting this experience and then that, again never making fundamental decisions that give their lives thrust and direction. They are moved by the play of circumstances on them. They are creatures of the wishes of other people. They do not take a basic responsibility for their own lives or the lives of others. Such people sooner or later become bored; they must continually seek new experiences to fill the emptiness of their lives.

B. *The Crowd*

Kierkegaard saw the same kind of evasion of responsibility and of true humanity in the phenomenon of the crowd. He was one of the first radical critics of "mass man." The basic reason for Kierkegaard's attack on "the crowd" is that the individual man loses himself in the crowd. He cannot be the individual he is called to be. Immersion in the crowd, in the mass of whatever kind, is loss of self; it is evasion of responsibility. The individual no longer makes the decisions that shape his life. The decisions are made in the crowd, by the crowd; his life is shaped for him. The crowd is dehumanization. What makes man human is lost. He becomes only a "number"— one among many. Man becomes anonymous in the mass.

"A crowd in its very concept is the untruth, by reason of the fact that it renders the individual completely impenitent and irresponsible, or at least weakens his sense of responsibility by reducing it to a fraction."[1] The individual in the crowd becomes a conformist. He does what others do; he thinks what others think; he feels what others feel. He is swept along by the tide. Such an analysis lies behind Kierkegaard's attack on the press and "public opinion." Mass communication and the public opinion shaped and controlled by it erode individual responsibility. It weakens or destroys the risk of standing up for the truth.

Becoming fully human, realizing personal existence, is something individual. It is inward. It can go on apart from, and in spite of, all external factors, though it is undermined by anything that would take away individual responsibility. For this reason Kierkegaard had no patience with the democratic political and social movements of his day. Changes in political or social structures, he believed, do nothing to bring about the inward change that is demanded if man is to become fully human. They do not change man's inner becoming and may destroy man's sense of responsibility for his own personal life. But Kierkegaard also attacked the bourgeois, or European middle-class, values. The bourgeois style of life is absorbed in things, in the everyday, in creature comforts. The bourgeois is the conventional. It is a life of business. Middle-class men have an ethics, but it is "a short summary of the police ordinances; for them the most important thing is to be a useful member of the state, and to air their opinions in the club of an evening."[2]

"The majority of men turn aside precisely where the higher life should begin for them, turn aside and become practical, 'man, father, and champion bowler.' "[3] So far as religion goes, the bourgeois does not and cannot really know God.

"In order really *to love* God, it is necessary to have *feared* God; the bourgeois' love of God begins when vegetable life is most active, when the hands are comfortably folded on the stomach, and the head sinks back into the cushions of the chair, while the eyes, drunk with sleep, gaze heavily for a moment toward the ceiling."[4]

C. *The Church*

The church in fact can be and usually is part of the crowd phenomenon. In the latter part of his life, Kierkegaard attacked the state church of his day. He attacked Christendom in the name of New Testament Christianity. Christianity—in the churches—had made itself a way of evading becoming fully human, of becoming truly an individual. The churches and the clergy have turned Christianity into something easy, so easy that everyone can be called a Christian. The clergy are just as worldly as anyone else. Christians become complacent, self-satisfied. What is more, they grow so contented that finally they do not realize how far the life of the church is from the Christianity preached in the New Testament. In his attack on

Christendom, Kierkegaard called for simple honesty.
Recognize our condition, he said. Admit how far we are
from what we pretend to be. This is the first step if we
are to introduce Christianity into Christendom.

Kierkegaard's diagnosis of what is wrong with man, interpreted in traditional theological categories, is that man
is a sinner. Man is not what he is intended by God to be.
Man has shirked his responsibility to be what God has
meant him to be—an individual, a fully human self.

II. WHAT IS MAN MEANT TO BE?

The goal for man, as understood by Kierkegaard, can be
described in a number of different ways. It is becoming an
individual, or as we might say today, realizing *personal*
existence. It is becoming a Christian, for this finally, for
Kierkegaard, is what full personal existence entails. It is
—to put it another way—to become a subject, a self. Kierkegaard has still other ways of describing man's end as
man, but the point of all of them is to indicate that man
can only be *on the way*, moving toward this goal, that the
goal is never possessed except in the moment. Man must
be continually in the process of "becoming" in the direction of the fully human life. Such a goal is a moving goal,
and man is understood in process terms as man on the way,
as man becoming. His movement is a movement out of
initial freedom, by free decision, toward increasing
freedom.

Kierkegaard develops his understanding of the fully
human life out of a very careful and subtle analysis of life
as man actually lives it. Part of this analysis is involved in
our description of what is wrong with man. The basic
thing that is wrong with man is that he is failing to become
what God intends him to be. He is not fully a self, fully a

person. And there are many, many ways in which man fails in this regard. Man can lose his identity and integrity in a crowd, or by being a spectator or observer, never really involved in life, or by being a floater or a taster. Such people are not really selves at all, because they do not make the fundamental kind of decisions about their lives that would give their lives direction and thrust, that would constitute them as selves in the very act of consolidating an integrity through decision.

A. *The Stages on Life's Way—the Aesthetic*

The movement toward what man is meant to be can be described, then, as a movement away from this absence of integrity, identity, selfhood; away from inertia and decisionlessness. Kierkegaard understood that life could be lived with a number of basic orientations, or stances. He called these basic ways of life or styles of life, "spheres of existence" or "stages on life's way." What stage or sphere a man belongs to depends on what is dominant in his way of life. The stage we have been describing as we have talked about what is wrong with man is what Kierkegaard called "the aesthetic stage." Such people do not really live seriously. To begin to live seriously, to make fundamental decisions, already puts one in a higher stage. One moves away from the aesthetic toward a higher degree of freedom through the free act of decision. The next basic style of life Kierkegaard called the "ethical."

B. *The Ethical*

Although each style of life or stage or sphere may contain a number of different substyles or variations, there is nevertheless a generalizable character. Those who exist at the ethical level have realized the seriousness of life. They have made and continue to make important decisions that shape their future and their relations to others. These are people who have some ideals in life. They realize that there is a basic difference between good and evil action and they strive to live for the good. They conceive of the good as defined by certain standards of behavior which apply to everyone. They try to live by these rules.

This mode of life represents an important advance over the aesthetic. These people, because they decide, have a center of decision within—a self. They are "freer," because freedom means decision leading to action. They have begun to live life at a more intense level of subjectivity than those at the aesthetic level.

C. *Religiousness A*

A third and fundamentally new level of life begins when a man realizes that the universal ethical demands— the "Law," in Biblical language—are not binding on him. He comes to see that God has a unique, personal, and individual relationship to each man that transcends or goes beyond the norm that is said to apply to all men. He now gives up living by the "rulebook" to live at the higher level demanded by his private and unique relationship to God. The new demand is that he have an absolute relationship to the Absolute and a relative relationship to all things relative in his own life. This is Kierkegaard's transcription of what it means to say that the demand upon each one of us is to seek the Kingdom of God *first*.

The person who lives at this level of life (and Kierkegaard calls it Religiousness A) finds God in his own inner life. A God relationship is possible from man's side. To live in this relationship means, so the individual discovers, *in-*

finite resignation, suffering, and *guilt.* That is, the individual who strives to have an absolute relation to the Absolute and a relative relation to all things relative finds that this means giving up his attachment to all things he ordinarily is devoted to. He must infinitely resign himself—retreat from attachment to all these relative goods—family, friends, comforts, health, wealth, reputation. He finds that this is indescribably difficult. If it is to be done, it must be done to him. He must be transformed and he cannot bring this about himself. And to the extent to which it happens it means suffering—the suffering of a change wrought against the grain of his own basic inclinations. When he finds that this is the demand upon him but that he cannot really bring it off, he sees himself as guilty.

The whole process, for Kierkegaard, is a further step in the right direction. Such a person is more of an individual, more of a self than the one who lives in the ethical sphere. His self-awareness is greatly intensified—by the struggle, by the suffering, and above all, by his sense of guilt. He is more of a self and a freer self because he has made a much more difficult and far-reaching decision; and it is decision that constitutes self. It is decision that increases and expresses man's freedom. Such a person lives with greater intensity, with greater passion, and with greater inwardness. He is more of a subject. He is further along the way to *becoming* an individual.

D. *Christian Existence*

Is any further deepening of self-awareness possible? Is there any further dimension of self-actualization, of freedom, inwardness, subjectivity? For Kierkegaard the fourth and highest level, or the deepest dimension of existence is the Christian life itself. When a man appropriates the Christian truth, he has true self-understanding. He sees that his guilt is guilt before God. It is sin, and he is a sinner. His recognition of himself as a sinner means that he recognizes what his true state is, that there is an infinite qualitative difference between him and God. He sees that he has, through his own action and attitude, created an abyss between himself and God and that he can do nothing about it.

The individual's realization of his true condition, his being stripped of all his pretensions and attempts at self-security, are just the ground in which he becomes receptive to God's grace, in which he can receive God's gift of faith. When his new receptivity makes faith possible, God can restore his integrity, can give a new unity to his becoming—a new self, a new kind of being. To become a Christian means to reach this stage of life's way and to maintain the newly given integrity by every new decision in faith. There is no resting-place. There is no security, no finality to any moment of decision. Man continues to live on this knife-edge, deciding and ever again deciding for faith.

Such is the basic structure of Kierkegaard's understanding of man's life. It is but the skeleton. Kierkegaard's own writings fill in with an incredible richness the particularity of life in each of the spheres. Furthermore, his whole point is that to understand this intellectually is of no avail. To understand intellectually without appropriation, without *living* in one's categories, is to remain in the arrested state that he calls the aesthetic stage. Kierkegaard's whole authorship and his manner of addressing his reader is an attempt to move the individual reader to appropriation, to decision. Decide now! These are the options; tomorrow may be too late.

E. *The Root of Man's Trouble*

Kierkegaard's general diagnosis of man is that he has lost his potential integrity, his unity. He lives a life in bondage; he is not free. Another way to characterize life apart from personal existence in the Christian dimension is to say that man is "in despair," he is a guilty sinner; he is filled with anxiety. How does this happen? How did man get into this condition, according to Kierkegaard? He believes that we can understand *how* this happens—though we cannot say why. We cannot give a causal analysis, just because man gets into this mess through the misuse of his own freedom. The trouble begins because man is anxious.

Why is man anxious, or under what conditions does man become anxious? Man becomes anxious, says Kierkegaard, as he faces his own potential freedom. When he faces his own future, there are so many possibilities open to him. If he chooses one, he will not be able to choose others. Poised before choice, he is fearful of losing what he has and what he is, for what he might have and might be. He is drawn both forward and backward at the same time. Like the man on a high tower he has the sense of wanting and of not wanting to leap. This is the dizziness of freedom, and it is anxiety. Anxiety arises in the insecurity before one's own freedom.

What does man do in the dizziness of his own freedom? He seeks security, and thereby he refuses faith, refuses to trust. Instead he tries to secure his own life, perhaps by retreating to a life lived in imagination, perhaps by trying to take command of his own life—depending on *his own* intelligence, *his own* health, *his own* strength. Or he may put his confidence in someone else or in some institution—someone who will tell him what to do. Or again he may give himself up to a life of sensuous indulgence, trying to obliterate from his awareness his own responsibility and the demand that he choose. He may be drawn into a crowd and become a mass man. These are some of the ways man may attempt to secure himself, to annul his consciousness of freedom, to evade responsibility.

Such patterns of behavior draw man into bondage. They do not finally overcome his anxiety, and yet at the same time they delimit or obliterate his freedom. They also represent the introduction of disunity into man's own inner being. He is in a state of disequilibrium. The bondage of sin is a kind of inner disunity or disintegration. Such a condition, whether felt as such or not, is what Kierkegaard calls despair. The pattern of healing is the process of reunification, the restoration of equilibrium and unity. In one of his works Kierkegaard talks about it as "purity of heart" —the capacity to will one thing. Kierkegaard's understanding of this process is that man cannot bring it off by himself. In his bondage he has lost the power to exert his freedom with integrity. He cannot heal himself.

III. The Path to the Goal Ends with Christ

The answer to this condition finally is Christ. Christ is the one who reveals to us what we are—sinners. And he brings the power of healing—first, because he does disclose us to ourselves so that we see what we really are, in such a way that we are ready to accept healing because we realize that we can do nothing of ourselves; second, because he also shows us what God is—that God is *for* us, that he forgives us. When we accept God's forgiveness, we act in faith. We acknowledge God as God. In this moment of acknowledgment we are restored to integrity; we receive a new self. In that moment and for that moment we are free. But this freedom must be renewed in every moment by a new decision. We are in continual danger of slipping back—of losing our integrity again.

A. *Faith*

Life in faith is not easy. It is not easy in the first place because it means seeing ourselves as we really are, alone with God—sinners. And this self-disclosure, as well as the acknowledgment in faith that God is for us, that he forgives us, means believing something that is in obvious contradiction to our reason. This contradiction Kierkegaard calls the absurd, the paradox. The absurd, the paradox, is Christ. Christ is a paradox, is the absurd because he is both man *and* God. Certainly no one relying upon his reason would believe this, Kierkegaard says. God and man are opposites. To say that God became man is rational absurdity. It is like saying black is white. What is more, the real challenge of faith is to know and believe this—to appropriate it in the face of the same conditions as the first followers of Jesus. When they "believed," they knew nothing of the glorified Christ, the Easter Christ. What they saw was a poor carpenter's son. Jesus was obviously a man, and of humble birth and background as well. To be sure, he was a good man, but he associated with the social outcasts, the sinners and the publicans, the people of skid row. Further than this, he would have appeared to many as a radical, as one who wanted to upset the established order of things, perhaps even revolutionary. He was not approved by the religious leaders. His work was a threat to the government, so some at least thought. And with all this, he claimed to be God—or at least his followers came to believe that God was present in his person. Doesn't this strike any reasonable man as absurd? Isn't it paradoxical that the Eternal should become temporal, that God should walk around in human flesh? What man "in his right mind" could believe this? Yet this is what some of his contemporaries believed. And this is the stumbling block to belief that each one of us faces if we would become contemporary with Christ. We must become such contemporaries and believe, says Kierkegaard, *if* we are to become Christians.

B. *Voluntary Suffering* "chief mark of Christian life". S.K.

But this is not the end of the difficulty. *If* we take this step, and have faith, a certain kind of life will follow. The chief mark of the Christian life, as Kierkegaard understood it, is voluntary suffering. Those who follow Christ must imitate in their own way and time his pattern. They must live a life for others, a life that embodies love and truth. What, asks Kierkegaard, happens to persons who live this way under the conditions of human existence? What happened to the first Christians? They were martyred. They suffered. So will it ever be, thought Kierkegaard. The truth is crucified by men—whether in our day it is the truth of radical justice or the truth about what must be done if men are to have peace. Love is forever on the scaffold. A Christian must not only believe. He must willingly be ready to suffer for the truth and for love. Kierkegaard's proof that Christendom had denied the Christian faith was that the clergy, the lay people, and the institution were comfortable, acceptable—so much so that everybody is a Christian and finds this tag an easy, respectable one to live with.

Did Kierkegaard claim that man could simply and straightforwardly assume this kind of stance toward existence? Did he claim to *be* a Christian or to be an exemplary Christian? The answer to all of these questions is negative. Christianity is not easy. It might even be said to be too much *for us*, and Kierkegaard did not claim to *be* a Christian. He did, at the end, come to think of himself as becoming one. But we must be honest about it. Certainly it is not easy. Certainly this business of Christian faith is not something that we can bring off "under our own steam." But with God all things are possible. All things work together for good to them who love him. This is Kierkegaard's reiterated theme. What finally *can* man do?

C. *Prayer*

Kierkegaard's answer, echoed both in his teaching and in his personal life, is prayer. Prayer is the means by which man initiates, nourishes, sustains, and indeed endures this process of becoming a Christian in his own life. What is demanded in prayer is absolute trust, absolute openness, absolute sincerity. Our task is to become transparent before God in all our weakness and all our hope. Prayer, says Kierkegaard, does not change God, but it makes it possible for God to change us. And such change wrought by God is the only path to fully human existence.

7: *Martin Buber —*
Man in Dialogue

MARTIN BUBER has been one of the most significant
religious thinkers of our period. He has exerted
more influence on Christian thinking than any other Jewish
philosopher in modern times. The list of Christian theologians who have paid homage to Buber includes the masters
of our day (the Niebuhrs, Tillich, Heim, Brunner, Barth,
Berdyaev, Marcel). Indeed, his ideas have spilled over
into the spheres of education, literary criticism, psycho-
therapy, and political philosophy.

Buber was born in 1878 and lived most of his early life
with his grandfather at Lemberg in Galicia. Under his
grandfather's influence he discovered the Hasidim, a
Jewish protest movement that was to affect greatly his
own interpretation of life. He died in 1965.

Buber studied at the Universities of Vienna and Berlin,
wrote his thesis on Christian mysticism, became active in
Zionism, and was appointed to a newly created chair of
Jewish philosophy at the University of Frankfort. His
university teaching was ended with the rise of the Nazis
to power. From 1933 to 1938 he taught in Jewish schools
helping to strengthen the identity and courage of his people. He then became professor of social philosophy at
Hebrew University in Israel. He retired in 1951, then lectured in England, the United States, and elsewhere out-

side Israel, extending the understanding of and interest in
his profound thought.

The reader of Martin Buber's classic work *I and Thou*
will surely notice a difference in tone and direction in comparison with the work of our other authors. Buber, though
he does not neglect the negative side of the human situation, seems much more interested in exploring the positive
constructive dimensions of human experience. In this work
he introduced the fundamental insight that permeates all
his later work. This insight is that a man may be oriented
to his world—to nature, to man, and to the products of
human creativity—in two basic ways. The crucial question in individual life and in culture is which of these
orientations will be dominant and controlling. Both are
important and necessary for human fulfillment; but if
one is dominant, human life will be impoverished; if the
other is dominant, the fully human life becomes possible.

I. The Two Basic Attitudes or Orientations

The two basic attitudes that one may take to what is
other than himself Buber called *I-Thou* and *I-It*. An individual may regard the other as a "Thou" or as an "It."
These are the crucial distinctions in Buber's understanding of man, and they lead to his further distinction between a life of monologue and a life of dialogue.

Perhaps the easiest way to get at the meaning of Buber's
distinction is to look at your own experiences. How have
you been treated by other individuals? Have you sometimes been treated as a thing and sometimes as a person?
The first kind of treatment would belong to Buber's I-It
dimension, the second to the I-Thou. A high school student
once explained the difference in these terms: "My mother
treats my dog like a dirty old shoe that gets in her way. I
treat him like a member of the family."

Buber, of course, went much farther than pointing to the distinction. He analyzed it, showing the important differences between the two ways of addressing or responding to the other. For example, when I treat the other as an It, the relationship might be described as that of a subject to an object. The other is an object to me. This means, says Buber, that what happens in such a relationship really happens within me. I have the relationship, so to say, in my control, in my experience. I can ignore what I want to about the other. I control whatever of myself I let enter into the relationship. I may only be interested in the other with a part of my being—what I *see* in him, or what I *will* for him, or what I *think* about him. He is for my experience and my use. I act toward him with a part of my being and I am interested in only a part of his being. Furthermore, the relationship is one way—it goes out from me to him.

In the case of an I-Thou relationship I am related as a subject to a subject, as a person to a person. What happens in the relationship is not in me, or in him; it is in the "between." Further, the relationship is not one-way—it is mutual. I enter the relationship with the whole of my being and relate to the whole of his being. The experience is not just mine, it is "ours." I am not interested in "using" the other; the relationship is for itself.

Though the "I" is one of the poles in each of the relationships, for Buber they are really different kinds of "I." The I of the I-It relationship he calls the I of individuality. The I of the I-Thou relationship he calls the I of personality. Individuality makes its appearance simply by being differentiated from other individualities. A person comes into being, however, by entering into relations with other persons. Every man is both kinds of I. A man is more or less personal. Buber illustrated the difference by pointing to the kind of "I" that Jesus and Socrates were, in contrast to the kind of "I" that Napoleon possessed.

II. THE TWO CONSEQUENT WAYS OF HUMAN LIFE

Depending upon which of the basic orientations to the other is dominant, a man leads a life of *monologue* or of *dialogue.* One of the elements in this contrast is the distinction between what Buber called "seeming" and "being." In dialogue the relationship proceeds from what one truly is. It is a relationship of "being." In monologue there is pretension and hypocrisy. One is interested in the impression he is giving to the other of what he is. In relationships of seeming the individual is concerned with the image the other is getting of him; he therefore contrives his looks, his speech, to create the image he wants the other to have. Here interaction is one of appearances. The individuals are not communicating their real being.

Another distinction important for differentiating monologue from genuine dialogue is that which Buber draws between the role of the propagandist and the educator. A relationship in which one tries to impose himself, his opinion, and his attitude on the other, even if he wants the other to think the result is really his own, represents the role of the propagandist. The kind of manipulation that is that of the advertiser or the salesman or the politician stands in the way of genuine dialogue. The attitude and action of the true educator is different. He too wants to affect the other, but he wants to do this by helping the other to unfold something that is really there in the being of the other. "He cannot wish to impose himself, for he believes in the effect of the actualizing forces—that is, he believes that in every man what is right is established in a single and uniquely personal way."[1] Not imposition, but unfolding is the mark of dialogue.

In genuine dialogue I try to overcome the inadequacy of my perception of the other one. I try "to make him present." For Buber this means that one must regard the other as *the very one he is.* I try to become aware of him as different, essentially different, in the definite and unique way that is peculiar to him. And in so doing I *accept* him in his difference. I affirm him. I *confirm* him, even though I may think him wrong. I accept him for what he is and affirm his freedom to become what he would become.

All of this implies a heightening of the awareness of the other. I must try to experience him as a whole in his concreteness. This kind of awareness runs counter to an analytical dissection of the other. I do not try to reduce the other to an abstraction ("He is a neurotic") or to a stereotype ("He is a Jew"). Rather, I try to be aware of just this individual in his uniqueness and concreteness. The only way this can be done is through a cultivation of sensitivity to the other and through the use of one's imagination to "go over to the other side" and to put oneself in the other's place and see and feel the world from his perspective.

For genuine dialogue one must not only make the other present; one must be fully present in the relationship oneself. One must not hold a part of himself back from the relationship. One must be willing to express oneself without reserve. This does not mean, I think, that one always says everything; but dialogue is a relationship in which one is *willing* to be completely open. Sometimes silence itself is an important part of genuine dialogue. In dialogue the partners genuinely speak to each other; they intend to share out of the depths of their own being. In monologue, men talk past each other; they are centered in themselves, not in the relationship.

To distinguish between these two modes of life, these two ways of existing, is of crucial importance. The one, if it is dominant, leads to a kind of subhuman life. The other opens up the possibility of what is authentically human, for the truly human is not to be found in the isolated individual: it is to be found in the meeting of man *with* man. Moreover, as we shall see, for Buber such understanding is filled with religious implication. It is God who makes possible such meeting, and it is God who is present at the depth dimension of every human meeting. In order to comprehend what Buber means here we must examine more closely how it becomes possible for the individual to move toward a life of dialogue.

III. The Inner Life of Man Moving Toward Dialogical Existence

A. *Wholeness*

An I-Thou relationship and the life of dialogue demands inner unity. The "Thou" can be spoken only with one's whole being, and such wholeness where nothing is held back means unity. This is perhaps another way of saying that such an individual has abandoned "seeming."

In contrast to inner unity there is inner division. For Buber what causes such inner division is evil, and the inner division itself is what evil or sin is. Sin, he says, is living divided and unfree. It is either decisionlessness or lack of direction and what is done in such a condition. For Buber, evil is not the result of decision, for real decision is not partial but is made with the whole being. Evil, we should note, is not something built into the nature of man (except as a possibility), nor is it ineradicable:

The man with the divided, complicated, contradictory soul, the divine force in its depths, is capable of . . . binding the conflicting forces together, amalgamating the diverging elements.[2]

But unification is never final. Again and again man moves away from it, and again and again it must be restored. It is interesting to note that Buber does not regard anything in man as being ineradicably evil. What appears to be evil —some of his urges or impulses—are not such in themselves. They need not be eliminated or repressed. They need rather to be drawn within the more powerful unity and made to serve the good.

It is a cruelly hazardous enterprise, this becoming a whole. . . . Everything in the nature of inclination, of indolence, of habits, of fondness for possibilities which has been swashbuckling within us, must be overcome, and overcome not by elimination, by suppression. . . . Rather all these mobile or static forces, seized by the soul's rapture, plunge of their own accord, as it were, into the mightiness of decision and dissolve within it.[3]

B. *Direction and Destiny*

The process of the unification of the self is closely related to the individual's finding his destiny and direction. The direction that needs to be discovered has two aspects: toward the person, which is purposed for one's self, and toward God. Direction is apprehended through one's inner awareness of what he is meant to be, for this is what makes it possible for one to make a genuine decision. One has "direction" when he has a sense of his destiny—when he has heard his "call" and when he has answered. Put another way, Buber would say a "Thou" speaks through events calling me to respond as an I to a Thou. We are continually being "addressed" by the events that happen to us. If we really listened to the language of events, we would hear the "word" addressed to us. We would sense in these happenings a meaning *for us*. We would hear a "call"; we would sense the meaning of our own uniqueness.

What we hear when we listen to what is emerging from ourselves in our own meeting of our world is our destiny— our unique vocation or direction within the common vocation or direction toward the eternal Thou.

C. *Decision and the Turning*

Once one has become aware of direction and destiny, decision is the next step. The name of the act of decision in its last intensity is "teshuvah" in Hebrew, which may be translated the *turning* or *reversal*. In reality, every particular decision may really be an expression of the decision, a part of the turning, the new movement in a single direction which is both the direction toward the person purposed for one and the direction toward God. The turning is really an answer to God's address:

In the infinite language of events and situations, eternally changing, but plain to the truly attentive, transcendence speaks to our hearts at the essential moments of personal life. And there is a language in which we can answer it; it is the language of our actions and attitudes, our reactions and abstentions; the totality of these answers is what we may call our answering, and for ourselves in the most proper sense of the expression.[4]

IV. GOD AND MAN'S LIFE IN THE DIALOGICAL MODE OF EXISTENCE

God, of course, is present for man, addressing him, calling him to the new life of dialogue in all the events of his life; but when the life of dialogue has come into being for the person, then God is present in a new way. In *I and Thou*, Buber writes:

Every particular Thou is a glimpse through to the eternal Thou; by means of every particular Thou the primary word addresses the eternal Thou. Through this mediation of the

Thou of all beings fulfillment, and nonfulfillment, of relations comes to them: the inborn Thou is realized in each relation and consummated in none. It is consummated only in the direct relation with the Thou that by its nature cannot become It.[5]

What Buber is saying is that in our human I-Thou relationship we also meet God. God is "there" as the source of personal being and its depth.

A further important implication of Buber's view is that it is foolish to try to seek God in some special way—in mysticism, or by trying to cultivate special rites and practices. God is already "here." Buber writes:

I know of nothing of a "world" and a "life in the world" that might separate a man from God. What is thus described is actually life with an alienated world of It, which one experiences and uses. He who truly goes out to meet the world goes out also to God.[6]

To go out to meet the world "truly" is for Buber to "hallow the everyday." God is not to be met in some special place but in the concreteness of the everyday.

If you explore the life of things and of conditioned being you come to the unfathomable, if you deny the life of things and of conditioned being, you stand before nothingness, if you hallow this life you meet the living God.[7]

In this sense for Buber, as for the Old Testament and for many Christians, religion as a special sphere of life is not real religion. "The realer religion is, so much the more it means its own overcoming. It wills to cease to be the special domain 'Religion' and wills to become life. It is concerned in the end and not with specific religious acts, but with redemption from all that is specific. Historically and biographically, it strives toward the pure Everyday."[8]

From this point of view nothing is really profane. What is profane is simply what has not yet been sanctified. Everything is waiting to be hallowed, for there is nothing so crass or so base that it cannot become material for sanctification. Redemption is thus seen not as redemption *from* evil, but redemption *of* evil. What is important is the way in which we meet the things that happen to us everyday—whether or not we develop a genuine relation to the people with whom we live and work, "the animals that help us, the soil we till, the materials we shape, the tools we use."

What one is called upon to do is to help God by loving his creation in his creatures, by loving it toward him. "People who love each other with holy love bring each other towards the love with which God loves his world."[9]

V. Man and the Social Order—Community or Collectivity

What kind of relationship exists between man and man —whether fulfillment is nurtured or thwarted—for the members of a society, depends on the dominant orientation of the social order. "In our age," says Buber, "the I-It relation, gigantically swollen, has usurped, practically uncontested, the mastery and the rule."[10] We stand, in fact, in the midst of crisis.

For the last three decades we have felt that we were living in the initial phases of the greatest crisis humanity has ever known. It grows increasingly clear to us that the tremendous happenings of the past years, too, can be understood only as symptoms of this crisis. It is not merely the crisis of one economic and social system being superseded by another, more or less ready to take its place; rather *all systems*, old and new, are equally involved in the crisis. *What is in question therefore, is nothing less than man's whole existence in the world.*[11]

What Buber meant by "the crisis" can be expressed in various ways. He meant that we have been moving steadily away from the kind of social order that could nurture dialogue. Both Communism and capitalism have broken down community and substituted mass-oriented, collective patterns of life. More and more, in both social orders, what Buber calls "the centralistic political principle" has subordinated the "decentralistic social principle." If we would understand Buber's social thought, we must look at the contrast between these two principles and between community and collectivity.

The political principle stands for coercive order and for centralization. It is most clearly seen to be operative in totalitarian societies; power becomes concentrated in a centralized state. But in our time it is omnipresent.

The crucial thing . . . was not that the state, particularly in its more or less totalitarian forms, weakened and gradually displaced the free associations, but that the political principle with all its centralistic features percolated into the associations themselves, modifying their structure and their whole inner life, and thus politicized society to an ever-increasing extent. Society's assimilation in the State was accelerated by the fact that, as a result of modern industrial development and its ordered chaos, involving the struggle of all against all for access to raw materials and for a larger share of the world market, there grew up, in place of the old struggles between States, struggles between whole societies. The individual society, feeling itself threatened not only by its neighbors' lust for aggression but also by things in general, knew no way of salvation save in complete submission to the principle of centralized power; and in the democratic forms of society no less than in its totalitarian forms, it made this its guiding principle. Everywhere the only thing of importance was the minute organization of power, the unquestioning observance of slogans, the saturation of the whole of society with the real or supposed

interests of the State. In the monstrous confusion of modern
life, only thinly disguised by the reliable functioning of the
economic and State-apparatus, the individual clings desper-
ately to the collectivity. The collectivities, so he thinks, can do
that, and he is all too willing to let himself be deprived of
personal responsibility: he only wants to obey.[12]

As a result, the most valuable of all goods, the life of man
with man, gets lost in the process.

In contrast to the centralistic political principle the decentralistic social principle is the principle of inner cohesion, collaboration, and mutual stimulation between the
"little societies" which make up the larger order. It restores genuine communal life and seeks to nurture quality
in the lives of the individuals. A social order dominated
by this principle does not try to standardize the whole; it
tolerates the emergence of elements of spontaneity and
the internal dynamism and diversity that are indispensable
to a genuine society.

Man in a collectivity is not man with man. "Collectivity
is not a binding but a bundling together. . . . Community
. . . is the being no longer side by side but *with* one another. . . . Collectivity is based on an organized atrophy
of personal existence, community on its increase and confirmation in life lived toward one another."[13]

For Buber the kind of social order seeking to organize
itself according to the decentralistic social principle is
what he calls *religious socialism.* Such a socialism is built
up through the renewal of the "little societies"—the basic
associations for common life and work in which, beyond
the family, man finds his roots and belonging. It is built
up through the creation of new modes of such association
which work together to foster life according to the social
principle. Buber calls for the rebirth of the "commune" or

of the cooperative. "On this," he says, "hangs the whole fate of the human race."[14]

By the cooperatives Buber says he means "the subjects of a changed economy: the collectives into whose hands the control of the means of production is to pass."[15] In an extended critique of Marx's thought Buber makes it clear that what was wrong with Marx was that he was willing to sacrifice almost everything to the centralist political principle. The fulfillment of this view in the Soviet regime has resulted, says Buber, in "a mass of socialistic expostulations, no Socialist form at all."[16] For Buber, there doubtless must be centralization—"but only so much as is indispensable in the given conditions of time and place."[17] There must be an unwearying scrutiny of conditions in light of the claims of community, for community is continually exposed to the depredations of centralist power.

The development of a social order based on real community would be fulfillment of the primary aspiration of all history.

The primary aspiration of all history is a genuine community of human beings—genuine because it is *community all through*. A community that failed to base itself on the actual and communal life of big and little groups living and working together, and on their mutual relationships, would be fictitious and counterfeit. Hence everything depends on whether the collectivity into whose hands the control of the means of production passes will facilitate and promote in its very structure and in all its institutions the genuine common life of the various groups composing it.[18]

For Buber, the formation of this kind of society making possible the nurturing of genuine community is a religious task, because genuine community is where the life of dialogue can take place. "Religious socialism means that man in the concreteness of his personal life takes seriously the fundamentals of this life: the fact that God is, that the world is, and that he, this human person, stands before God and in the world," where all things are to be hallowed.[19]

8: *Reinhold Niebuhr —*
Man as Sinner

REINHOLD NIEBUHR was born in 1892. Brought up in a pastor's home, he attended Elmhurst College and Yale Divinity School. Assigned to a pastorate in Detroit he found pastoral work and preaching amidst the problems of an industrial center a radical challenge to the liberal theology and the moralistic ethic he had hitherto accepted. Influenced by Marxism, he helped to organize the Fellowship of Socialist Christians. In 1928 he became a member of the Union Theological Seminary faculty where he continued to develop a prophetic Christian social concern based upon a new undertanding of Biblical faith and its view of man.

More than any other American thinker in the thirties, forties, and fifties Niebuhr helped to change the theological climate in this country. Beginning as a liberal and a pacifist he moved theologically to the right and socially and politically to the left. Central to his interests have been the problems of Christian ethics, and his impact has been great on secular thinkers in the area of political and social problems as well as on his fellow churchmen. On the theological side his greatest contribution has been his analysis of man's nature and destiny.

I. What Is Wrong with Man?

Niebuhr's view of what is wrong with man is very close in many respects to Kierkegaard's, which we examined earlier. It is close both because Niebuhr derives certain aspects of his thinking from Kierkegaard and because they both are rooted in certain orthodox and Reformation modes of understanding human nature. Yet they differ in important respects, both because Kierkegaard's understanding of the psychological dimension of man's inner life is more complex and subtle and because Niebuhr is interested in the social implications of his understanding of man in a way that is missing in Kierkegaard.

For Niebuhr, as for Kierkegaard, what is wrong with man is that man is a sinner. To say this is to say that he sees man in the light of his relationship to God, for sin is a theological category. Man's condition as a sinner (as distinguished from the fact that he commits particular "sins") is described by Niebuhr in a number of different ways. It is "man's unwillingness to acknowledge his finiteness."[1] It consists of his "efforts to transcend his proper state to become like God."[2] It is separation from God in the sense that man by his self-assertion denies what is his proper relationship to God. This he does because he is self-centered; he is inescapably egotistical. Rejecting the orthodox tradition that such a condition is somehow inherited, Niebuhr treats the story of Adam as a myth which gives a true account of what is universally true about man. There was not a particular time in history when a first man "fell," but there is "original sin" in the sense that there is a universal and inevitable inclination or tendency in man to deny his limitations.

Niebuhr's understanding of *why* man becomes a sinner

is grounded in Kierkegaard's interpretation of the nature of anxiety, and anxiety (the fact that man becomes anxious) is related to his understanding of man's existing at the juncture of nature and spirit. To say this is to point to man's freedom. Let us examine these notions.

Man's freedom has its source in the fact that he is "spirit" as well as nature. To say that man is spirit points to his capacity to transcend himself, that is, to stand off from both himself and his world—to reason—to objectify possibilities and to objectify himself. In this situation man always envisages possibilities that are greater than his capacities, and this makes him strive for a perfection that is beyond his capacities. He becomes anxious. In his freedom as he faces the many possibilities he may also feel insecure, and this feeling of insecurity prompts anxiety.

Anxiety is not sin—but for Niebuhr as for Kierkegaard anxiety is the precondition of sin. In such an anxious condition man either asserts himself beyond his limits, and this is the more basic condition of sin, or he tries to escape the insecurity of his freedom. In neither case is his sin really "necessary" or inevitable. It is an act of his freedom, and therefore he is responsible for his condition as sinner, according to Niebuhr.

For Niebuhr the covering term for the first form of sin—that in which man acts in ways that, in effect, deny his limitations—is _pride_. The second form, in which man tries to escape his freedom's insecurity, is _sensuality_.

A. Sin as _Pride_

1. Pride of power. Pride of power takes two forms. It is the pride of those who assume their self-sufficiency and self-mastery and think they are secure. It is also the pride that is the motive of the lust for power. Greed would be

an example of this will-to-power. But of course, says Niebuhr, will-to-power leads in a vicious circle. The more one
gets, the more one has to lose; and so the more insecurity
threatens and more power is demanded to overcome it
and so on.

2. Intellectual pride. This is the kind of pride that people take in the thought that their knowledge or their
beliefs are superior. Such people cannot see the limitations
of their own grasp of the truth or the partiality of their
perspective.

3. Moral pride. Moral pride is involved in intellectual
matters too. "Moral pride is revealed in all 'self-righteous'
judgments in which the other is condemned because he
fails to conform to the highly arbitrary standards of the
self."[3]

4. Spiritual pride. This religious or spiritual pride issues
from moral pride when one's moral pride attempts to claim
divine sanction. Our judgments, our views, are claimed as
the truth of God. "This is done when our partial standards
and relative attainments are explicitly related to the un-
conditioned good."[4]

All of these forms of pride have their root in self-
centeredness. They are modes of self-love. We think too
highly of ourselves. We fail to acknowledge our finitude
and our limitations. They are ways of exalting ourselves
and by this, denying our proper creaturely relationship
to God.

B. Sin as Sensuality

Sensuality is, for Niebuhr, a form of sin. In one sense it
is derived from pride. Sensuality can be a way of self-
glorification through physical pleasure rather than through
power, knowledge, or virtue. But the individual may be-

come aware of his sensual self-love and feel guilty. In consequence he tries to escape the sensual love of the self through sensual abandonment to another or, for example, in drunkenness.

II. What Man Is Meant to Be

That man is not meant to be a self-centered egotist becomes clear in his sense of conflict between what he is and what he could be. There is still enough "health" left in man to enable him to perceive that he is not "healthy." Further, the vision of Christ, for Christians at least, heightens the sense of contrast. Niebuhr talks about the "image of God" in man and man's "original perfection." These are terms that refer to Adam's state before the Fall in Biblical and traditional thought. For Niebuhr, they do not, any more than the story of the Fall itself, refer to any literal historical events. This Biblical story is a myth which tells a truth to man about himself. What these terms do refer to is a structure of possibility which defines what man is meant to be, what his fulfillment is. Essential man includes his natural endowments and determinations expressing themselves in harmony. It includes the freedom that he has in his capacity for self-transcendence, fulfilled in a life of faith, hope, and love. Man's original righteousness was present at no particular time in history; it is present in the moment before the self acts. It is present when the self regards its earlier action and "knows itself as merely a finite creature among many others and realizes that the undue claims which the anxious self in action makes result in injustices to its fellows."[5]

One might say more summarily that love is the vision of health that "even a sick man may envisage." For Niebuhr, as we shall see, love is action in relation to the other in

which all self-regard is eliminated. But such love would
mean the elimination of anxiety and neither non-self-
regarding love nor freedom from anxiety are simple possibilities for human existence. Niebuhr regards as naïve and
utopian those within Christianity who think they can
really live according to such norms.

The norm for man—what man is meant to be—is then
disclosed in man's own experience at the point where he
becomes aware of a lack. One might say that the norm is
disclosed as a law which man is not fulfilling and which he
discovers he cannot fulfill under his own power. This
awareness of the norm is "heightened" in the confrontation
with the Christ. Christ and his cross clarify both the human predicament and the human goal. "He is what I am
essentially, and therefore what I ought to be."[6] The cross
shows the radical character of man's own self-contradic-
tion and yet at the same time shows man the nature of the
love that represents fulfilled manhood.

III. Christ and the Fulfillment of Life

According to Niebuhr and to the Reformation interpretation of Biblical teaching, man is "saved"—his inner contradiction is healed, he is brought to fulfillment by grace—
the grace of Jesus Christ. Grace is the freely given love of
God in Jesus Christ. It is understood by Niebuhr as _wis-
dom_ and as _power_. What do these terms mean to Niebuhr?

In Christ, wisdom is given. This means that in him the
"true meaning of life" has been disclosed. In Christ, power
is given. This means "that resources have been made
available to fulfill that meaning."[7] Grace is the power of
God _over_ man—the power in which he through mercy and
forgiveness completes what man cannot complete. Grace
is the power of God _in_ man (traditionally given through

the Holy Spirit indwelling in man) by which man receives new resources for life and finds his life transformed.

Niebuhr believes that this view of grace as pardon (or forgiveness) and as power (new life, new selfhood) is true to the Biblical teaching. In fact he develops this view in a striking exposition of Paul's verse in Galatians (ch. 2:20), "I am crucified with Christ: nevertheless I live; yet not I, but Christ liveth in me: and the life which I now live in the flesh I live by the faith of the Son of God, who loved me, and gave himself for me."[8] The crucial question, says Niebuhr, is not whether this is what the Bible teaches but whether it makes any sense in relation to modern man's experience. In particular, the question is whether the notion of forgiveness and continued living out of forgiveness makes any sense for contemporary man.

Niebuhr's answer is that it does make sense. No matter how high or how far the Spirit leads man to new life, "the conscience remains uneasy." One never finally achieves "peace." In the development of new life "some contradiction between human self-will and the divine purpose remains."[9] What we live out of, then, is faith and forgiveness. There are infinite possibilities of organizing life from "beyond the centre of the self," but every possibility is paralleled by a possibility of "new evil."[10]

It is important to grasp Niebuhr's significant point. Fulfillment in Christ, so far as life in this world is concerned, does not mean that man becomes sinless. Niebuhr would, moreover, explicitly deny that the realization of *agapē* or selfless love is ever a simple possibility for man:

Christ in us is not a possession but a hope. . . . Perfection is not a reality but an intention. . . . Such peace as we know in this life is never purely the peace of achievement but the serenity of being "completely known and all forgiven."[11]

Niebuhr's understanding of the misery and greatness of man, that he is both sinner and redeemed, has brought what might be called an element of *realism* into his interpretation of the concrete activities of men, and a lack of sentimentality about the church and his fellow Christians. Though there is much more that could be said about his understanding of the inner contradiction in man and the work of Christ for him and in him, we need to look at the implications Niebuhr draws from his understanding for the larger scene of human activity, for it is in this realm that his thought has been particularly influential and provocative.

IV. MAN IN SOCIETY

One of the clear implications of Niebuhr's understanding of the nature of man is that his sin (pride, self-centeredness, and self-interest) will be observable wherever men are. It will be found in group and social life as well as in the individual and in the individual's relations to other individuals. It will be found, then, in politics, in the economic realm, in the church. The further implication is that we ought not to have any illusions either about motives (our own or those of other groups) or about the possibility of any simple solutions to the problems that arise at this level. Niebuhr is therefore highly critical of all sentimentalisms and utopian views about society. On the other hand, he sees that one of the most significant problems is that of how to deal with power in the interaction of social groups—whether this be the power of nations, economic classes, or political groups within a nation.

A second implication is that the norm of love—if it is the norm for human life—must somehow be made relevant to the social scene. If love is not a simple possibility (and it is always subject to corruption), then some method of relating it to the human social issue must be found other than the effort embodied in the injunction, "All you have to do is love your neighbor as yourself."

3. A third implication is that just as there are always possibilities of evil inherent in human freedom, so there are indeterminate possibilities for a greater good beyond the present existing situation. Niebuhr has often been painted as a pessimist because of his vigorous attention to man as sinner; but it must be pointed out that, both in his teaching and in his own role as activist on the social and political scene, he has forcefully called attention to the possibilities beyond the present which more nearly approximate what is ultimately desirable in a given situation. As he says at one point: "There are no limits to be set in history for the achievement of more universal brotherhood, for the development of more perfect and more inclusive human relations."[12] Yet he would allow no one to think that even these possibilities will be pure and untainted by the tincture of self-interest.

A. *The Relevance of Love*

It might be said that it is exactly the first and the last of the implications that provide the means by which Niebuhr charts the relevance of the norm of love for decision and action. The law of love is not something extra to be added to our morality and social relations. Rather "it is the guiding principle of them."[13] Love is the guiding principle in the sense that it is the criterion of judgment helping us evaluate the relative merits of one path of action rather than another. Love is the guiding principle in that it obligates man to find the best possible proximate pattern for solving social problems.

For Niebuhr this means that love moves man to seek justice and to be sensitive to injustice. Niebuhr writes:

> To know both the law of love as the final standard and the law of self-love as a persistent force is to enable Christians to have a foundation for a pragmatic ethic in which power and self-interest are used, beguiled, harnessed and deflected for the ultimate end of establishing the highest and most inclusive possible community of justice and order.[14]

It is important to see that in his view of justice and its relationship to love Niebuhr is repudiating two traditional Christian positions which have been held in certain circles. He is repudiating the separation of love and justice made by those who suggest that there are two realms—the one in which justice is the goal and the other in which love is relevant. Niebuhr would hold that love and justice are not separable in this way. Further, Niebuhr is repudiating the view that justice can give place to love if only people become more loving. Justice remains necessary, for even those who are most loving may be just the ones who will abuse power, since in their love they may claim to be certain of what is best for others.

B. *The Achievement of Justice*

The achievement of justice involves *order, equality*, and *freedom*.

Order. Order and social cohesion are necessary for the very existence of a society and so also of justice itself. Too great an emphasis on order, which may take the form of resistance to change in the name of order, may, however, also subvert justice. It may be only a defense of privilege.

Equality. Equality is a dynamic notion for Niebuhr. It is, first of all, a kind of principle of criticism that points to the various corruptions of self-interest, the inequalities promoted by those who have power. It means also equality of opportunity and equality of treatment before the law. It is, says Niebuhr, the most logical "application of the ideal of love in a world in which life is in conflict with life."[15]

Equality as a pinnacle of the ideal of justice implicitly points towards love as the final norm of justice; for equal justice is the approximation of brotherhood under the conditions of sin.[16]

Just as was the case with the principle of order, a balancing of values may be necessary. There are some who would emphasize equality to such a degree and in ways which may destroy order entirely and so prevent even an approximation of justice. Just so too, equality may be emphasized in ways which destroy freedom.

Freedom. Freedom or liberty is also a regulative principle of justice. Men's "highest good consists in freedom to develop the essential potentialities of their nature without hindrance," writes Niebuhr in *An Interpretation of Christian Ethics.*[17] But liberty stands in tension with equality. Some groups will push for greater equality, and in order to achieve it will limit freedom. Others will push for greater freedom and in order to achieve it are willing to produce great inequalities.

Since justice involves all these elements and since each of these has group power (whether political, economic, or national groupings) striving for or against one or another of them, Niebuhr argues that justice demands not only a balancing of these elements but a balancing of power within the society. There is no absolute and unchanging pattern. What justice means in a given time and place depends on the best possible balancing that is workable in that situation, but the movement toward justice is one that gives man freedom with increasing equality. Moreover, love itself demands that schemes for justice be accepted only provisionally, lest present structures of justice stand in the way of the realization of still fuller embodiments of the law of love.

V. NIEBUHR'S POLEMICS

Much of Niebuhr's writing and speaking has had a polemical bent. His own thought has developed in debate against alternative positions either in history or on the contemporary scene. We are not interested for our purposes in the full variety of Niebuhr's opponents, but since we have tried to summarize something of Marx's and Freud's thought about man, it may be valuable to see what Niebuhr has had to say about them.

A. *Niebuhr on Marx*

Niebuhr has, from his days in Detroit as a pastor, been deeply influenced by Marx and Marxism. For a number of years he termed himself a Marxist Christian. He was never a Communist and was increasingly critical of the Communist movement. At the same time, however, he was deeply appreciative of the Marxist unmasking of the illusions of liberalism and the belief that the ills of the economic order could be met by tinkering with the capitalistic structures. In the period of the Depression and in Niebuhr's experience in the industrial struggles of the Detroit days, the Marxist analysis of the power structure and conflict coincided with his own realistic appraisals. A radical reconstruction of the economic order was called for, he thought, and for this reason he had no use for what he regarded as the palliative measures of the early New Deal. Niebuhr never seems to have accepted Marxist utopianism or the exclusive interest in the proletariat. He was critical from the beginning and became increasingly critical of the abuse of power in communist states. In the light of his political realism he has long advocated a tough-minded policy of containment of Communism.

In a recent article he has summarized some of the criticisms which are to be made of Marx and Marxism. Marx's analysis of the class structure of technical society was too simple and his estimate of the resources of capitalism to avoid catastrophe was false. The increasing misery of the poor did not occur. Communism was led to establish a monopoly of power in order to realize justice, whereas an equilibrium of power is the first pre-requisite of justice. The reason for this was the false equation of man's self-regard with greed; there are clearly many other forms of the lust for power. False too was the derivation of egotism from a particular institution (property), which led to the illusion that its elimination would remake man.[18]

B. *Niebuhr on Freud*

Niebuhr deeply appreciates Freud's realism about man, his break with the kind of optimism that thought human reason could control the impulses and guide man to ever more inclusive rational ends. His criticism has to do with Freud's failure to do full justice to man's transcendent freedom of spirit. This failure leads Freud to locate the pursuit of self-interest in the id rather than to see self-regard as present at every level including the ego. A similar point is expressed in his criticism of Freud's view of the super-ego, which he calls a completely social-pressure view. Such a view makes "inexplicable the ability of the self to defy the community, whether it does so in its own interests or in the name of a higher value than that which the community embodies."[19]

Another equally fundamental criticism lies in Niebuhr's judgment that Freud's attempt to explain man's behavior in naturalistic categories leads to a distortion and over-simplification which could only be corrected by seeing man in historical terms. In a way, this is another way of pointing to Freud's denial of the freedom possible through self-transcendence. The conclusion to which Niebuhr is led is that Freud's type of thinking has increasing limitations when one attempts to apply it to the world of politics or to other areas in which the historical factor is so decisive.

9: *A Personal Viewpoint*

U P TO THIS POINT our discussion has centered on various views of man which contend for his loyalty in
the marketplace of ideas. The author has purposely attempted to keep his own viewpoint in the background in
order to allow the reader, indeed, in order to encourage
the reader to respond for himself. Each of us must, however, take his own stand, and I would not wish to leave my
own views hidden behind a mask of apparent detachment.
My own conviction is that man is *meant to become a center of freedom and of love*.[1] What is wrong with man is
that he resists this direction. He turns away or retreats
from such fullness of life. The unfulfilled man is the "arrested" man, the man in bondage, the man unable to love.

I. BECOMING

To say that man is meant to become a center of freedom
and of love means that everyone has within himself this
potentiality. Such becoming is the realization of the image
of God in man. It is to do God's will, for God's will for man
can only mean that he should become what he was created
to be. It is to actualize what one essentially is or what one
is in his deepest potentialities. To say that man's task is to
become is to point to the dynamic character of that task.

Indeed it is to point to the dynamic character of man himself. Man is not a static entity. He is a becoming, developing, growing, moving mode of being. His being is constituted by his becoming. He is dynamic process. As long as man exists, he becomes; when he ceases to become, he ceases to be. To go on to say that man's task is to become a center of freedom and love is to indicate a direction for this becoming. It is to assert further that there is no end point, no static point of rest or of achievement at which the individual himself or some other can say that the goal has finally been reached, that no more remains to be done. There is a direction, but the direction is not an end point. It is a moving goal. The center of freedom and love is itself a moving center. Freedom and love reach out in ever-widening circles. They reach down in increasing intensity and depth. They are themselves creative, productive of novelty, of new possibilities of extension and depth.

To say that man's life task is to become a center of freedom and love is also to point to the risk involved, the threat that is ever present from every side. To cease to become is to cease to be. It is death in the physical sense. To cease to become a center of freedom and love is to cease to be in the spiritual sense. Failure here is the route toward meaninglessness, boredom, nihilism. What is wrong with man, then, is that his becoming is arrested. He resists moving ahead. His development is held back. He does not have the courage to risk himself to the future. He draws back either in fear or in contentment. He may be self-satisfied or defensive. Shut up within himself, he withdraws behind walls of a static existence. He will not venture far out. All of us know those who live this kind of life. Satisfied with the old, afraid of the new, it may be our way of life too.

II. A CENTER

The second term in our vision of man is "center." Man is created to have a center, but he is to *be* a center of freedom and love. To speak of the centeredness of man is to speak of his unity, his consistency, his self-identity. All of these are relative terms. Each of us is more or less unified, more or less consistent, more or less possessed of self-identity. It is obvious, too, that some individuals are not well integrated. Some are divided by inner conflict. Some men are, as Kierkegaard put it, a colony of incoherent desires and contradictory impulses. When C. S. Lewis began his movement in the direction of the Christian faith, he examined himself for the first time "with a seriously practical purpose." "And there I found what appalled me; a zoo of lusts, a bedlam of ambitions, a nursery of fears, a harem of fondled hatreds. My name was legion."[2]

Others have their "center" on their periphery. They float along on the surface of life, playing one role one time and place and another at another time and place. There is neither observable nor felt consistency underlying their roles. Such people shift with every wind of doctrine. They are creatures of others' wishes and desires or of their own changing needs. Some may find that they have no inner core of selfhood of their own. They depend for their self-definition on the commitments of others. So, a few years before he died, the novelist F. Scott Fitzgerald wrote of his own failure to achieve integrity:

After a long time I came to these conclusions, just as I write them here:

(1) That I had done very little thinking, save within the problems of my craft. For twenty years a certain man had been my intellectual conscience. That was Edmund Wilson.

(2) That another man represented my sense of the "good life," although I saw him once in a decade, and since then he might have been hung. He is in the fur business in the Northwest and wouldn't like his name set down here. But in difficult situations I have tried to think what *he* would have thought, how *he* would have acted.

(3) That a third contemporary had been an artistic conscience to me—I had not imitated his infectious style, because my own style, such as it is, was formed before he published anything, but there was an awful pull toward him when I was on a spot.

(4) That a fourth man had come to dictate my relations with other people when these relations were successful: how to do, what to say. How to make people at least momentarily happy. . . . This always confused me and made me want to go out and get drunk, but this man had seen the game, analyzed it and beaten it, and his word was good enough for me.

(5) That my political conscience had scarcely existed for ten years save as an element of irony in my stuff. When I became again concerned with the system I should function under, it was a man much younger than myself who brought it to me, with a mixture of passion and fresh air.

So there was not an "I" any more—not a basis on which I could organize my self-respect—save my limitless capacity for toil that it seemed I possessed no more. It was strange to have no self—to be like a little boy left alone in a big house, who knew that now he could do anything he wanted to do, but found that there was nothing that he wanted to do.[3]

A more amusing example of the same failure to be a self is to be found in one of Jules Feiffer's cartoon sequences.[4] A boy, "Danny," is pictured. He says:

Ever since I was a little kid I didn't want to be me. I wanted to be Billie Widdledon. And Billie didn't even LIKE me. . . .

I walked like He walked. I talked like He talked. I signed up for the same High School He signed up for. . . .

Which was when Billie Widdledon changed. He began to hang around Herby Vandeman. He WALKED like Herby Vandeman. He talked like Herby Vandeman. . . .

And then it dawned on me that Herby Vandeman walked and talked like Joey Haverlin and Joey Haverlin walked and talked like Corky Sabinson.

So here I am walking and talking like Billie Widdledon's imitation of Herby Vandeman's version of Joey Haverlin trying to walk and talk like Corky Sabinson. And WHO do you think Corky Sabinson is always walking and talking like?

Of ALL people—

Dopey Kenny Wellington—

That little pest who walks and talks like me.

Not all struggle on to self-identity and self-awareness. Some are so torn by contradictory and conflicting forces within that no clear direction of movement is possible for them. Still others, once possessed of both a sense of their own identity and a degree of inner coherence, may under the impact of great internal or external stress disintegrate, fall apart.

Internal unity and its behavioral manifestations is not simply a matter of the formation of stable and habitual patterns. It is rather the reflection of a unifying intention, a stable system of values, an underlying purposiveness. Single-mindedness must emerge out of double-mindedness, and ultimate single-mindedness is what Kierkegaard called "purity of heart." Central to such coherence and unity is the individual's view of himself, of his own self-identity, which is related to his view of his world. The perception of the self is the complement of the perception of the world. Yet not everything that looks like single-mindedness is true purity of heart. There are those who are highly unified, who are consistent, integrated, purposive. They are centered selves indeed. They have their disruptive drives under some kind of control. Their behavior is highly predictable just because they are so unified and consistent, but the unity and consistency are built out of defensive rigidities. Such persons are relatively incapable of change—of movement. They remain what they are. These people are an example of arrested development, but they also may be said to be in bondage—bondage to themselves and to the relatively inflexible patterns that have become the substance of their personal being. In contrast to this kind of personal unity there is another, which does not inhibit or choke off personal becoming. These people are also consistent and possessed of inner coherence, but in addition they have a certain flexibility and adaptability. They are predictable as to the type of response they are likely to make but not so much to their detailed behavior. There is likely to be an element of surprise, for they are capable of a creative response to life and to their world. Such people are open; they can become more than they are. They can learn from their experience. They can learn how to enter into the lives of others. They can allow others to enter into their lives. There is in them the ground for a life of freedom and love.

Centeredness, self-identity, inner coherence, consistency —all these are prerequisites to becoming fully human. No individual becomes a person capable of freedom and love without such centeredness. Yet the qualitative differences between types of centeredness must be kept clearly in mind. Centeredness is not enough. A bigot, or an aggressive destructive individual, may have a clear sense of his own identity; he may have a high degree of internal consistency; and his external behavior may be all of a piece, yet he is capable of neither freedom nor love.

III. OF FREEDOM

Normative becoming—becoming fully human in the Christian sense—is a becoming which increases one's freedom and his capacity to love. Freedom, like centeredness, is a relative matter. An individual has either more or less freedom. Persons are more or less in bondage. Some men are prisoners of their past. Perhaps the most crucial forms of such bondage are destructive dependency relationships and guilt. Both kinds of bondage are disclosed in the form of the self the individual has developed. Destructive dependencies are a kind of constriction and rigidity in the self. Guilt is both a heritage and the contemporary presence of inner conflict, of the self divided against itself. In Kierkegaardian terms guilt is one of the forms of being unable to "will one thing," to be an integrated, unified self. Guilt, of course, may be seen wherever we have done an injury to the fabric of human life, where through commission or omission we have broken the web of relationship that nurtures, sustains, and restores the human good. No more vivid account of the extent and subtlety of this condition of man has come to my attention than Kenneth Fearing's poem, "Confession Overheard in a Subway."[5]

You will ask how I came to be eavesdropping, in the
    first place
The answer is, I was not.
The man who confessed to these several crimes (call
    him John Doe)
        Spoke into my right ear on a crowded subway
        train, while the man whom he addressed (call
        him Richard Roe) stood at my left.
Thus, I stood between them, and they talked, or
    sometimes shouted, quite literally straight
    through me.

How could I help but overhear?
Perhaps I might have gone away to some other strap.
      But the aisles were full.
Besides, I felt, for some reason, curious.

"I do not deny my guilt," said John Doe. "My own,
      first, and after that my guilty knowledge of
      still further guilt.
I have counterfeited often, and successfully.
I have been guilty of ignorance, and talking
      with conviction, of intolerable wisdom
      and keeping silent.
Through carelessness, or cowardice, I have shortened
      the lives of better men. And the name for
      that is murder.
All my life I have been a receiver of stolen goods."

"Personally, I always mind my own business," said Richard
      Roe.
      "Sensible people don't get into those scrapes."

"Guilt," said John, "is always and everywhere nothing
      less than guilt. . . .
I have always, at all times, been a willing accomplice
      of the crass and the crude.
I have overheard, daily, the smallest details of con-
      spiracies against the human race, vast in their
      ultimate scope, and conspired, daily, to launch
      my own.
You have heard of innocent men who died in the chair.
It was my greed that threw the switch.
I helped, and I do not deny it, to nail that guy
      to the cross and shall continue to help.
Look into my eyes, you can see the guilt.
Look at my face, my hair, my very clothing, you
      will see guilt written plainly everywhere.

Guilt of the flesh. Of the soul. Of laughing
     when others do not. Of breathing and
     eating and sleeping.
I am guilty of what? Of guilt. Guilty of guilt, that
     is all, and enough."

Guilt may, however, take a still more pervasive form,
and perhaps in this form it is universal. There is a kind of
inner duplicity in man that the existentialists have particularly pointed to, which has the quality of guilt in it since
it is the radical violation of what man is meant to be. It is
the denial of his potential unity and integrity. Camus has
called attention to this in his novel *The Fall*. This novel
is the story of a former Paris lawyer, Jean-Baptiste
Clamence, who in a long monologue tells his story to another man who is unidentified. Clamence has been a successful lawyer; he had done many good deeds, but then
little by little he is brought to a kind of self-discovery. He
finds that he really is a "fake," a hypocrite. He has used
his modesty, his humility, his apparent virtue, in his own
interests. He begins to see for himself that he was not what
he pretended to be or what he appeared to be. Finally,
he tells how he has become what he calls a "judge-
penitent," one who spends his time telling his confession
to others, revealing his own situation, confronting them
with his own condition "as a mirror for themselves." We
see another expression of this human condition in Sartre's
description of "bad faith."[6] Bad faith is different from a lie.
In a lie, the liar knows the truth that he hides. In bad
faith, he hides the truth even from himself. Such guilt
makes one a prisoner of the present as well as of the past.
We are in bondage, too, when we are self-satisfied as we
are, when we are merely what others want us to be, or
when we simply reflect the social and cultural conditioning
of our time, our class, our little group.

The problem of guilt points sharply to the depth of man's bondage, but just as there are dimensions of bondage, there are dimensions of freedom. The degree of an individual's freedom seems to depend upon a number of factors: the range of possibilities open to the individual, the adequacy of his perception of these possibilities and of the structures of reality within which such possibilities can be realized. Anything that limits the actual range of possibilities decreases an individual's freedom. Anything that distorts his perception of either the possibilities or the structures of reality also decreases the individual's freedom.

The wide range of human freedom can readily be seen through a number of contrasting examples. Compare the child with the normal mature adult. Contrast the alcoholic or neurotic or psychotic with a psychologically healthy individual. The child's range of possibilities and his perception of both the possibilities and the structures of reality are both relatively limited. The same would be true of the alcoholic, the neurotic, and the psychotic. Not only is the range of their possibilities actually limited, since they are bound by various forces beyond their control and indeed beyond their awareness, but their perception of the structures of reality may be more or less distorted. Furthermore, the alcoholic, the neurotic, and the psychotic may be so torn by inner conflict that they cannot be said to be centered selves at all. And centeredness is the presupposition of decisive self-determination. The child may possess a good deal of spontaneity, but even this may be lacking in the other three. Their behavior may often be more predictable, and it is perhaps this very predictability that makes the methodological assumption of determinism so effective and the apparent denial of freedom so substantial in the study of abnormal behavior.

Freedom is reduced when inner conflict threatens the centeredness of the individual or where duplicity and guilt warp the perception of self and reality. Freedom is reduced where the individual, by defensive maneuver, shuts out of awareness experience that might otherwise have rendered him "teachable" (to use Calvin's term) and thereby have opened up new possibilities for him. All of the conditions of freedom may be limited by both external and internal factors. Overpowering anxiety, guilt, despair, as well as the external influences of other persons, social, political, economic, and cultural forces, can threaten and diminish man's freedom.

On the other hand, whatever helps to extend the range of human possibilities, to move the individual toward a centeredness which remains open to change, helps to increase the individual's freedom. Some of the threats to human freedom are contingent, historical, circumstantial. They affect this man and not that one, in this situation and not in that. Other threats to human freedom seem to be written into the very nature of human existence itself. No man can have any final freedom from such threats until he can find release from the power of these threatening aspects of human existence which push him toward constant defensiveness and closure or toward despair and hopelessness. Unless man can know that there are possibilities beyond all that he can think and know, unless he can be freed from the distortions of his inescapable anxiety and guilt, unless he can somehow become aware of the ultimate depth and structure of reality which makes his own being and fulfillment possible, he can never be finally released from bondage into new life. While the freedom of Christ is not irrelevant to the more superficial and circumstantial dimensions of man's experience, it is absolutely critical with respect to the deeper dimensions of the human problem.

IV. And of Love

To the degree that an individual has freedom, to that degree he becomes capable of love. Love demands freedom, just as freedom demands a certain kind of centeredness. An individual who is capable of loving is capable of relating to another from his own center. This kind of relatedness which we call love cannot be forced. It must be a movement out of freedom which respects the freedom of the other and nourishes the freedom of both. The same kind of forces that inhibit freedom by distorting the perception the individual has of himself, of others, and of the real world also inhibit the emergence of love. Anxiety and guilt are disjunctive rather than conjunctive. They move a person against others, away from others, or if they turn a person toward others, the emerging relationship is likely to be that of unhealthy dependence or absorption. Centeredness and freedom do not guarantee that relationships to others will be those of love, but they make loving relatedness possible. Mature love does not issue from inner bondage or from self-destructive dependencies. It must be initiated in freedom.

While in their ultimate dimensions selfhood and freedom may coalesce, combine, perhaps become identical with love, there is no guarantee that at other levels they will even lead in the direction of love. Freedom, indeed, may be used in ways that oppose, resist, or even destroy love. Man may, in his freedom, act with hostility and destructive power against his neighbor. His aggressiveness may create patterns that undermine the possibility or fulfillment for others and that may even turn inwardly to destroy himself. Freedom may be used to separate man from man, to cut off the possibilities of relatedness. When such is the issue of freedom, whether in hostile action or in simple withdrawal from or blockage to potential relationship, the result is human loneliness. There is much that would lead us to diagnose loneliness as the elemental human condition under the circumstances of existence that many men face. Whether we listen to Paul Tournier describing the life of a secretary in Geneva:

". . . and so we bid you a very pleasant good night!" Often she used to turn on the radio in the evening, just as the program ended, in order to hear these few words, in order to hear a human voice wish her good night. Yet, she worked as a secretary of an international welfare organization. Her boss, a fine man, had dedicated his whole life to the battle against a social scourge. Many visitors from every country came to see him, but in the office they spoke only business. Never was there a word addressed to her as a person. Who she was, how she, a foreigner, had come to Geneva after many ups and downs, the sorrows that still deeply troubled her—nobody cared about these things. Her work was appreciated, and she received every courtesy, but to all intents and purposes she remained alone.

She lived in one of those great modern buildings, with countless one-room flats, where the neighbors' noises come from every floor. She knew none of those neighbors with whom she rubbed shoulders in the elevator daily, and they did not know her. She had no intimate friends. Her room was even in the same building where she worked. She rarely went out for any reason except for the odd hurried shopping trip. Before falling asleep, she would switch on the radio, ". . . and so we bid you a very pleasant good night!" It was a human voice, speaking *to her*.[7]

or whether we listen to Charlie Brown in *Peanuts:*

Oh, how I hate these lunch hours! I always have to eat alone because nobody likes me. . . . I wish that little red-haired girl would come over and sit with me. . . . I'd give anything to talk with her. . . . And she'd never like me, though. . . . I'm so blah and so stupid. . . . She'd never like me. . . . I wonder what would happen if I went over and tried to talk to her! Everybody would probably laugh. . . . She'd probably be insulted too, if someone as blah as I am tried to talk to her. . . . I hate lunch hour. . . . All it does is make me lonely. . . . During class it doesn't matter. . . . I can't even eat. . . . Nothing tastes good. . . . Why can't I eat lunch with that little red-haired girl? Then I'd be happy. . . . Rats! Nobody is ever going to like me. . . . Lunch hour is the loneliest hour of the day![8]

the human story is the same. And some have even seen the central intent of Christ's message as the destruction of the life of loneliness. Thomas Wolfe was convinced that loneliness was the central fact of human life. It was not rare or peculiar to men like himself. Rather he found that in the lives of all kinds of people there was a kind of inner suffering that was rooted in loneliness. It was to be found not only in the heights and depths of the poet's experience, but also in the life and sensitivity of the average man. Such loneliness, he thought, lies behind the hatred, the contempt, the mutual abuse and scorn which characterize so much of the human scene.[9]

If this be the human situation, love may be its only redemption. Love is a form of participation in the life of another. It is a sharing of oneself and an openness to reciprocal sharing by the other. In love one gives himself in such a way as to be open to sharing the other's hopes and fears, joys and sorrows. One gives himself but does not lose himself. Love is an act of freedom in which one loses neither freedom nor integrity. It is an act in which one responds to the freedom and integrity of the other. To respond means to be responsible for—to care for. Love is not so much reunion as it is communion, a being together. Being together is qualitatively a new kind of being, a distinct mode of being. In love I affirm the being of the other, but I also affirm my own being. I confirm our being-together. To love means to give up the *burden* of self, not to give up self. Those who are encumbered, who are burdened with self cannot be available to the other. They can neither be present to the other in wholeness, nor invoke the other's presence.

Love intends the good of the other, but the good of the other is not to be seen as excluding one's own good, for all good is social. Though love always intends the good of the other, it may not move to full mutuality, for love may not be reciprocated or it may not be reciprocated at the same level at which it is given. The parent's love for the child, the therapist's concern for his client, the doctor's care of his patient, the teacher's relation to his student, God's love for man—all these may be rebuffed, may be met with ingratitude, may be resisted. Or the other may simply be incapable of responding at the same level. Yet love intends mutuality. The intention of love is grounded in hope; hope that the child will one day be mature enough to reciprocate the love the parent expresses, that healing will restore the freedom to love, that the student may develop the capacities for full mutuality, that man himself will respond, turn toward God to love God with heart, and mind, and soul.

V. SUCH BECOMING IS NOT A SIMPLE POSSIBILITY

The goal for man, the meaning of full humanness, is the movement—becoming a center of freedom and love. Every aspect of life is relevant to this goal; every stage on life's

way may be related to it. Yet such becoming, which is also
the becoming of the Christian man and could be termed
growth in grace, is not a simple human possibility. Not
only is such movement threatened by the "accidents" of
one's personal history, i.e., by the contingent particularity
of the existence of each one of us, the influences that happen to have surrounded each of our lives, and that will
vary from person to person and place to place. Becoming
is also threatened by conditions that seem universal in
the human situation. Authentic selfhood, freedom, and
love are hard pressed from every side, from both within
and without. Existence has a tragic character, and becoming a center of freedom and love is a becoming in the face
of tragedy. It is a direction maintained against the grain
of circumstance. This is the reason that the cross has always been seen by the Christian as one of the marks of the
truly human life. The suffering of man for the good,
whether the good is the good of another or the good of
his own inward transformation, opens up personal and
social life to new ranges of meaning and value. Such suffering is the invocation of God's presence to work cre-
atively and redemptively on the human scene.

Direction can only have its source and power in trust
and hope. Active trust in the One whose reality underlies
whatever possibilities there are of personal being, of authentic selfhood, freedom, and love, is what makes man
able to live in the face of his own failures, the destructiveness, inertia, and unresponsiveness of others, and the resistance and intractability of the web of circumstance. It
is such trust that delivers man from ultimate despair even
in those moments when his Christian becoming seems
paralyzed and when forces over which he has no control
seem bent on the destruction of human values and on the

prevention of the emergence of a new and greater good. What stands in the way of man's movement in this direction is mistrust or the placing of one's trust in that which is an idol, i.e., in that which will ultimately betray one.

How does one move toward the kind of trust that brings reversal of direction and the freedom to love? The Christian answer is that it is the Christ who can so transform a man's life, though the Christ is not simply to be identified with or limited to the human historical Jesus. What happened to the first followers of Jesus must also happen to each one of us. If we try to get at this originating situation, we may come close to the meaning of this answer. Kierkegaard may have come closest to giving a clear characterization of that situation.[10] Those who saw Jesus as the Christ did not at first, he wrote, meet him as the risen and glorified Lord. They saw not the Christ who sits in glory at the right hand of the Father. Rather they saw a man, a lowly man, born of a despised maiden, his father a carpenter. His kindred people were of the working class. A lowly man, living in poverty with twelve poor fellows drawn from the simplest classes of society who were his disciples. He is shunned, hated, despised, and finally crucified. To be sure, he was good, compassionate, approachable by all and the servant of all, ministering and calling others to minister one to another. But the result of such a ministry was suffering.

And yet there were those who amidst all the others, when confronted by this incarnated goodness, and in contrast to the expectations of their people and their time, came to declare that in this man they had seen God. They came to comprehend that God was like this; that this is what God intended for men; that the reality disclosed in

his life and ministry was the answer to man's ageless
searching and questioning, that this reality alone was that
in which man could place his trust. In the midst of all of
the threats of man's life, in the face of the tragic character
of human existence—even this man's death on the cross—
these first Christians came to understand and feel the
power for healing, for fulfillment, and for the transmuta-
tion, if not the abolition, of tragedy through their encounter with Jesus. They found themselves in the hands of
a power not their own, of an otherness which spoke to
them in their situation, which grasped them and drew
them beyond themselves, remaking them in its image and
likeness, empowering them for their life in the world.

It is my conviction that having seen and felt this
presence in the events of Jesus' ministry, we can see it
again and again disclosed in the web of interpersonal relationships and on the plane of history. Or having experienced this presence in other ways, one might almost say
having confronted the Christ pseudonymously, one can
relate this experience to what took place in the rise of the
Christian movement. As Norman Pittenger says, for the
Christian faith, Jesus defines but does not confine God in
his relationship to the world.[11] This is, I think, what the
writer of the Gospel of John means in the opening verses
of his Gospel. The New Testament scholar C. H. Dodd
reads the Prologue in this fashion:

The ground of all real existence is that divine meaning or
principle which is manifested in Jesus Christ. It was this principle, separable in thought from God, but not in reality separate
from Him, that existed before the world was, and is *the pattern
by which, and the power through which,* it was created. The
life that is in the world, the light that is in the mind of man,
are what we have found in Christ. (My italics.)[12]

There is then, a mysterious good, a greater love, which was disclosed to man in Christ. The patterning of this same creative good can be found, I believe, in every experience of the emergence of new meaning and value beyond our control or intention. Such presence is found in the healing of the brokenness of human life which reaches beyond human contrivance. It is to be seen in the reclamation and redemption of evil, in the overcoming of error by truth. It is to be found also in the constant offer of new beginnings for personal and communal life.

In all such events God is present—incognito. Here we find the possibility that human loneliness can be overcome. We discover that we are not alone. The mysterious good, the greater love, is present with us and for us. And as each one of us ministers to another, helping to overcome the barriers of defensive separation, or as one of us is ministered to by another, we may come to say with Martin Buber:

Because this human being exists, in the darkness the light lies hidden, in fear salvation, and in the callousness of one's fellow-men, the Great Love.[13]

Because this person exists in this relationship—meaninglessness is not all and cannot be the real truth. We are not alone, for we are not our own.

10: *The Nature and Destiny of Man — Unanswered Questions*

Now that we have looked at man through the eyes of a number of his interpreters it may be well to draw together some of the basic issues and problems which such an analysis provokes, issues and problems that would remain with us even if we found one or another of the interpretations more satisfactory than the rest. Such a summing up may also lead to our further exploration of the problem of man's self-understanding beyond the introductory approach in this short book.

I. THE VARIETY OF INTERPRETATIONS

Perhaps the most obvious fact, so obvious that it stares one in the face as he looks over the preceding chapters, is the variety and the diversity in the understandings of man in Western culture. Still other ways of understanding man exist in our culture, and the fact of difference is important. If we ask *why* there are these basically different ways of understanding man's nature and his future, there are also varying answers to that question. The Marxist explanation of the existence of the Freudian point of view or the Freudian explanation of the Christian point of view would point to alternative estimates of the causal factors. Cutting across this variety of explanations, we could say that one clear reason for the variety is the kind of *evidence* the different perspectives consider. The sources for under- standing man are different. Huxley takes biological and anthropological evidence as determinative, though he has tried to use other materials as well. Freud has looked pri- marily at neurotic phenomena and at one aspect of human development. Marx looked to economic and political pro- cesses in their historical development. He was interested in the broader aspects of man's life rather than in the na- ture and development of the individual. Kierkegaard, on the other hand, was interested primarily in individual man. His interpretation of man is Biblical, but the Biblical interpretation is informed by and informs his analysis of the inner experience of the person. Buber's view may also be said to be Biblical, but, in contrast to Kierkegaard, he sees that the individual never becomes a person except in relation. The focus of his writing is on the interpersonal, though he is certainly concerned for the larger context of these relationships in society and culture. Niebuhr, too, is Biblical in the sense that he is rooted in the prophetic and Christological perspectives of the Old and New Testa- ments. But he is not bound to the Bible. The understand- ing of man's nature and destiny for which he argues is not true because it is in the Bible; it is true rather because it does, in fact, illuminate human experience better than any other. Teilhard is unique among our religious figures, since he blends the material from the natural sciences with a theological stance until he has a synthetic vision of the whole. My own view expressed in the preceding chapter can be characterized as a Christological perspective sup- ported and constructed with an awareness of the contribution of the psychological disciplines to an understanding of man.

These observations lead us to sharpen the question. Where are we to go for our understanding of man? Is any one of these areas of human experience sufficient? This is an especially important question for the Christian, for within Christian theology this issue is a matter of considerable controversy. There are, for example, within Christianity, the fundamentalists and the Barthians. Both would have us go to the Bible and to the Bible alone for our understanding of what man really is. The fundamentalists would tell us that the words of the Bible are God's communication to us telling us what man is, where he came from, and what his destiny is. If the Bible tells us that man was created in a certain way by God, then this is the truth about his origin. If the Bible tells us that hellfire or some kind of immortality is his destiny, then this is the truth about man's future. It doesn't matter what biological evidences or anthropological studies show about the evolutionary process. If these contradict the Bible, they cannot be true.

The Barthians, on the other hand, do not interpret the Bible so literalistically. The Bible is not, they think, intended to tell us about man at the same level as scientific investigations. What evolution or Freud or some similar viewpoint tells us about man, simply bypasses the crucial issue which exists at another level. Such information may be important for man's everyday life, for helping those who are emotionally disturbed, or for understanding man's place within the natural order, but it is useless or worse for telling us about the essential man, about what man really is, about his true significance, i.e., about his relationship to God. Such knowledge of man depends on our knowledge of the Word of God, which speaks to us through the words of the Bible, and this Word of God is Christ. We encounter Christ in the Bible (not just words about Jesus or some teachings of Jesus about this or that). There is a speaking of God to man through the Bible, a form of address that discloses to man that he is a forgiven sinner, that God is God *for* man. This is the important knowledge for faith. Psychological, scientific, sociological, literary, insights into man's existence are secondary and are of no importance for faith.

Not all Christian thinkers, by any means, come at the problem of man as do the fundamentalists or the Barthians. For some, like Teilhard, the matter of evolution is of tremendous importance if we are to understand man and his destiny. It provides the clue that helps us to understand how God works in nature and culture. For others, the understanding of man gained through the social sciences, through sociology, anthropology, psychology, has a positive contribution to make in supplementing and correcting earlier Christian interpretations. They too need criticism and correction, for they represent partial and time-bound perspectives. Some Christian theologians would say that such disciplines can help illuminate man's present condition, in traditional terms, man's condition under the Fall or man as sinner. These people would hold that such disciplines can make no contribution to the determination of what man ought to be, or to the question as to how he is to become what he ought to be. Other theologians see relevant insights in the so-called secular world even for these latter questions.

One of the important remaining issues, then, emerging out of these studies of man is that of the relationship of the Christian viewpoint to these others. Are the secular modes of understanding man simply to be rejected? Do they have an important contribution to make? If so, How can a Christian understanding of man take them into account?

II. THE PROBLEM OF LANGUAGE AND COMMUNICATION

Related to the question of the way in which the Christian perspective on man shall take account of non-Christian or secular views is that of how the Christian view is to be communicated. Of course, this is a wider issue than that of the doctrine of man. It concerns the expression of the whole of the Christian faith. What kind of language is to be used to express the Christian faith in such a way that contemporary man will not only understand what the faith is, but also be moved to see its relevance to the issues of life as they confront us in our day? It would be too simple to say that this is simply a question of the relation of Christians to the non-Christian segment of Western culture. It is internal to Christianity as well, for each of us is also a contemporary man.

With this issue we are at the heart of another controversy within Christian thought. There are those who believe that to restate the Christian faith apart from Biblical modes of thought runs the danger of, indeed will probably lead to, a loss of what is essential to the Christian position. Some of these are the literalists. Others who hold that we need to keep to Biblical modes of thought do so because they believe the dramatic categories of the Bible are alone able to do justice to the complexity of human experience. They would say that philosophical modes of thought inevitably lose something that is determinative for Christian thinking. Some of these, like Niebuhr, would resort to a kind of mythical method of theological analysis in which the great Christian myths are probed for the ever valid truth they embody. Even here, however, questions arise, and Niebuhr has been recently reported as having changed his mind about some aspects of our problem. "We cannot use any longer the language of the tradition if we want to communicate anything to the people of our time." It is no use, he now says, to "hurl the traditional symbols of Christian realism—the fall and original sin—in the teeth of modern culture," as he himself tried to do.[1] Such language is only misunderstood.

Others, like Paul Tillich, have tried to reinterpret the traditional categories in terms that are more comprehensible to modern men whose thinking has come under the influence of Marx and Freud. In place of sin he speaks of alienation and estrangement. Rudolf Bultmann calls for "demythologization," simply admitting that the three-story universe of Biblical men, with its demons and angels and the like, is no longer our world. Biblical notions are to be given an existential interpretation, meaning that they have to be translated into language that expresses something about man and his realization as an authentic self.

We need, then, to become clear on this question of language. Does a change in language necessarily mean a loss, or is some kind of translation indispensable both for communicating the Christian view of man and for relating it to other views of man present in our culture?

III. What *Is* Wrong with Man?

All the views we have analyzed assume that something is wrong with man. Men fall short of what they might be or of what they ought to be. Even Professor Huxley and Teilhard de Chardin, who seem to be the most optimistic of the figures we have considered, take some account of the problem of evil and acknowledge that man may fail to manage the processes of cultural evolution in a way that enables him to avoid his own self-destruction.

The crucial question that arises from a consideration of the various views is not only that concerning *what* is wrong with man but also that as to how man got into his predicament. This issue is important both with respect to the individual and to the society of men. These are important questions, because the answer to them conditions the answer to the question as to whether anything can be *done* about what is wrong with man, and if something can be done, what that something is.

The complexity of the answers to these questions raises another issue. Are different kinds of things wrong with man, which must be dealt with on different levels? The traditional Christian view that man is a sinner, whether interpreted literalistically through the assumption of a historical fall or symbolically as a description of the condition of every man, suggests so profound a predicament as to be beyond any human solution. So also does Freud's diagnosis of the human situation. In neither case can man help himself. He needs help from outside. For Freud, the individual's difficulties can be alleviated, but there is no final healing or salvation. For Niebuhr the outworkings of sin can be reduced as men struggle for justice under the judgment and forgiveness of the divine love they see in Christ. Not much is said by Niebuhr, however, about the transformation of the individual man into a better man, or into a man who is, in fact, less rather than more self-centered and egotistical.

In the case of Huxley and Marx, though the answers are quite different, man can, by changing the conditions under which he lives his life, bring about a fundamental change in the orientation of the individual. Buber, too, would seem to agree with this general position. Man has possibilities for good or evil, but the evil tendencies in him can be redeemed, can be taken up into the service of the good. And the conditions of the social order do affect the outcome; they block and promote the growth of the personal, and man can alter these conditions. Whether he does move in the direction of the person seems to be partly his responsibility and partly the effect of the grace that is inlaid in the folds of life. Kierkegaard sees the social order as either irrelevant or negative in its influence on man's becoming what he ought to be. This is largely an affair between God and man, and here man can only hold himself open to grace through prayer. God, then, works in him through the power of forgiveness to create faith and a new self.

The writers who take individual development in one form or another seriously, especially Freud and Kierkegaard, see the element of the personal history of the individual as of great import, for good or ill. Freud is the only one of the authors (though there are many others whom we have not studied) who takes what happens to the child with real seriousness.

To point to these distinctions may be enough to suggest unfinished business in moving toward an adequate understanding of man. May it be that there are, written into the very structures of human life, conditions that make it impossible for man to live without anxiety and which therefore prevent him from achieving on his own any simple realization of his potentialities as man? An adequate understanding would have to discover what these conditions are. Is Freud right in seeing that the ineradicable conditions are those of a conflict of instinct and culture or of life and death instincts within man? Or does anxiety arise in the face of man's freedom where self-consciousness makes him aware of his own unavoidable insecurity? Does anxiety always lead to pride and sensuality or does it also lead to other forms of self-loss and destructive inner conflict?

Further analysis would have to move to a very important practical problem. Why does inner conflict lead in some men to patterns of individual and group behavior that is so much more destructive than that of other men? Perhaps most of the views we have considered are oversimplifications. Freud's complex treatment of childhood and Kierkegaard's subtle analysis of the various kinds of options men do in fact choose suggest at least the range of the task we need to undertake. We doubtless need to trace the particular kinds of human character and social organization to whatever social and historical conditions there are that can be modified. Cross-cultural studies, for example, show that patterns of child-rearing or of institutional relationships do very greatly affect what a given individual in a society becomes. Such investigations may not lead to optimism about the human situation so far as man can alter it. Perhaps we will find that the course of human history has so enmeshed man in bondage that his capacities to modify his situation are very small indeed. Even in that case we will profit by knowing what a man *can* do. We may discover or have disclosed to us that even a life lived against the grain of circumstance and in suffering, if it is a life of love, is the very nature of man's highest realization as man.

IV. The Goal for Man

Considerations such as these lead us directly to the question of the fully human life and the problem of its realization. As we have seen, this issue has an individual and a social aspect. Though they are interrelated, each author has seemed to emphasize one or the other. Some have been interested primarily in the goal for the individual. Some have placed their emphasis on the goal for mankind or for a society.

Looking back over the views of the men we have been studying, we see that a number of them define the goal in a way that is somehow related to the notion of love. For Kierkegaard, one way of describing the Christian life is to talk about the imitation of Christ, the loving life that is willing to suffer voluntarily for the truth. For Niebuhr, the measure of man's life is also Christ and the love that was disclosed in the cross. Since man cannot actually live this way, love is for Niebuhr the norm and the motive in relation to justice. For Buber, dialogic existence might also be described as love in the form of mutuality. Teilhard saw love as the ultimate "force" holding things together and marking human self-realization in personhood. Freud speaks of human health in terms of being able "to work and to love." Marx and Huxley are more interested in the larger social and cultural realms, but insofar as Marx sees the goal as the overcoming of alienation, he too may be said to speak of love. Even Huxley wants to affirm the "unique importance of love in human life . . .," "indispensable for the full development of the human personality."[2]

Love is a covering word which may mean many things. What it is and what it does is somehow a clue to the meaning of human life. We need a careful consideration of the meaning of love in human life. Is love in its highest form simply selfless giving of the self to and for the other? Or is the highest form of love somehow transactional—mutual—seeking even if it does not find an answering response? Was Freud's conception of love too narrow? What is the relationship of what he meant by love to the love the others talk about?

We need to be able to find what releases love in human life and to discover the sources of hate and aggression. Are hate and hostility the return for lack of love? What does childhood experience have to do with the development of a capacity for love and hate? Do people become capable of love by being preached to? by reading the Bible? What is there in the religious community that could release people to love? What are the presuppositions of love? Are some people prevented from loving others by the kind of internal conflict they suffer from? Is love a static goal or a moving one? Does anyone experience an increasing capacity to love? Are those writers correct who assert that the problem of human fulfillment is not one of final achievement but of direction? What social, political, economic, and educational conditions best create the context for the nurture of the fulfillment of the individual in love?

V. THE WAY

We have analyzed a number of differing paths to human fulfillment. Some have said that man is what he is because the economic factors of production are organized in a certain way. If we would change man, we must change the structure of society, particularly the economic factor. Others have said that what we need most is an understanding of the processes that have produced and make human life possible, namely biological and cultural evolution. We need a new ideology based upon such an understanding, discarding the old, archaic, misleading ways of looking at nature and man. To the degree that we get such knowledge, so they say, we shall be able to control the processes of evolution and lead man to human fulfillment. Then there are those who say that what we must know is our past—the determinations of our internal history. Mere intellectual knowledge is not enough. We must appropriate this knowledge in our inner being. Though we cannot get rid of all conflict, we can at least have insight into it, an insight that will deliver us from its most destructive effects on us and on others. That is all we can hope for, and even to do this we must have the help of another who can draw out the insight into our own inner life that we need to be healed.

The religious writers agree: Life is such that man cannot reach the goal by thinking or by manipulating himself or society. Yet man is not alone. There is a reality that transcends the merely human, a reality that not only creates and nurtures human life but brings good out of evil and truth out of falsehood. Man, they say, must keep himself open and responsive to this good which he neither creates nor controls. He may, if he listens for its form of address and remains teachable, respond to it as he would to another person. Sooner or later, these men say, man must learn that the only path to the fully human life is through an openness to the future that can only be maintained through an active trust in the good which is not his own but which is yet his own good. Some would say that this "grace" is exclusively known in Jesus Christ. Others would claim that it is present and can be known in the whole realm of the interpersonal. Still others would say that once it has been known in Christ, its presence can be seen again and again at other points in personal and community life, perhaps in nature itself.

However this issue is resolved in the realm of personal experience there remains the wider social scene. The structures of society need to be looked at to discover what blocks the working of God's grace. Are there structures that could be re-formed and transformed through man's intentional activity so that human responsiveness might be nurtured and personal life fulfilled? In more traditional language, what *does* the Christian understanding of the Kingdom of God imply for the life of the church in the world?

Questions for Study and Discussion

CHAPTER 1

The purpose of the introductory chapter to these studies of varying interpretations of man was to increase our sensitivity to the implicit views of man that pervade our culture. It is difficult to know how powerful any one of them may be in influencing an individual's conception of himself or a community's view of expected and desirable behavior. Certainly there are some such images, imbedded in parts of the culture or in institutions, which seem to affect very powerfully even daily events reported in the press. An example would be the image of man that is imbedded in what is sometimes called "the southern way of life." Certainly one important function of any kind of study is the development of critical and reflective skills. The following suggestions and questions are designed to stimulate individual thought or group discussion.

1. Try to put into words two or three basic convictions about man which would be widely shared by most Americans at least at the verbal level. Where do these ideas come from? Do these convictions in fact guide the behavior of most Americans?

2. Take some popular magazine like *Life*, which contains a good deal of advertising. Try to analyze what view of man the people who write the advertising copy have. What kind of view of man are they trying to give to those to whom they are trying to sell their products?

3. What media in popular culture do you believe have the

most power in shaping our understanding of man? What kind of picture of man do they present?

4. Do you think that the various views of man conveyed in the popular culture ultimately cancel each other out or is there any common denominator that makes them in some sense support each other in their impact on all of us?

Suggestions for further reading: Mass Culture: The Popular Arts in America, edited by Bernard Rosenberg and David Manning White (a Free Press paperback) will be of interest as will the critical discussions in *Culture for the Millions? Mass Media in Modern Society,* edited by Norman Jacobs (a Beacon Press paperback).

CHAPTER 2

One of the basic issues evoked by Julian Huxley's evolutionary interpretation of man, both for Christian thought and for every other view of man, has to do with the significance of man's long biological history and his emergence as an "animal with culture." Christians need to ask: Can the phenomenon of evolution be ignored if we want to understand what man is and what he can become?

Another fundamental issue has to do with the meaning of evolution itself—either on the biological or on the cosmic level. Does it point to purpose—whether embodied within the process or somehow operating on the processes of nature yet not limited to these processes—or not? Most theologians ignore evolution. A few make it central to their understanding of man and God. Does it matter?

A further matter of importance is related to Huxley's view that earlier ideologies are archaic (whether religious, philosophical, or what). He thinks that we need a new world view and a new view of man. Furthermore, he holds that since the most reliable, indeed the only valid, way to knowledge is through the application of the scientific method, this new ideology must itself be based on what the sciences have discovered and can discover. These two issues—whether or not the older views are simply outmoded and whether or not there are other modes of knowing than that of the scientific method —need vigorous debate. Even if one disagrees with Huxley's point of view on these issues, the question still remains: What has theology (or philosophy or art or any other approach to the meaning of the world and human existence) to do with the new discoveries and theories of modern science?

1. What do you think most church people think about the relation of the evolutionary understanding of man's origins to the Biblical stories of the Creation in Genesis?

2. If the proportional relation of man's history to the existence of life is the thickness of a postage stamp to a monument sixty-nine feet high, what does this do to your view of man, his place in nature, and his possible future?

3. What do you think about Huxley's view of evil?

Suggestions for further reading: Huxley's views on religion are conveniently available in his *Religion Without Revelation* (Mentor Book). A very valuable discussion of the general problem of the relation of religion and science will be found in A. N. Whitehead, *Science and the Modern World,* Chapter XII (Mentor Book).

CHAPTER 3

Teilhard raises many of the same questions for his readers as does Huxley, but beyond this, it is interesting to try to sketch the similarities and differences between these two interpretations of the implications of evolution. What seem to you to be two or three major differences and two or three substantial similarities in their thought? Huxley commends Teilhard's views on evolution when he expresses himself as a scientist. What do you suppose he would be likely to say about Teilhard's religious perspective on evolution? What do you think Teilhard would say about Huxley's understanding of religion?

1. Read Col., chs. 1–2. How does the view of Christ in that letter seem to you to be related to what Teilhard has had to say?

2. In what way does Teilhard's understanding of man's future seem to you to be unrealistic, and in what way does it seem to be realistic?

3. How do you think Teilhard's views would be accepted in the churches if they were widely known? Would the people you know respond positively or negatively? Why?

Suggestion for further reading: Teilhard's *The Phenomenon of Man* (Harper Torchbook).

CHAPTER 4

A discussion of Marx's thought is of particular relevance, of course, because of the present East-West struggle, but Marx raises questions that are of more than contemporary interest. More sharply than any of the other authors we have considered, he poses the question as to the determination of the nature and meaning of man's life by its wider social context, centering attention on the economic organization of production. The larger implication of this view is obvious. Man can change the conditions of his life and so overcome those obstacles which cut him off from true manhood. Whether one agrees with Marx on his particular analysis or on his recommended solution to the human problem or not, this larger question remains. To what degree is the fulfillment of man as man determined by the way in which society is organized? What changes would have to take place to give man a higher degree of freedom and fulfillment?

Or to go to a deeper level—what actually produces the situation in which men exploit one another, in which aggression and hostility of man against man, group against group, nation against nation, tend to destroy some men's chances for the good life, and perhaps ultimately that of all men? Can this situation be altered?

Another issue that is of great import and which can be addressed apart from his particular analysis has to do with the significance of *work* in human life. What is the relationship between work and the fully human life? This is a matter that too few theologians and psychologists and philosophers have considered.

1. To what extent do you sympathize with Marx's condemnation of the conditions existing in capitalist industrialization as Marx saw it in history and in his own time? Should people be expendable in the way in which he described it? Why or why not? To what extent is this true in our society today? Why is the situation changed? Are there places in America today, or in other parts of the world, where the situation he described is still true?

2. As you survey the work situation in our society today, do men seem alienated from their work? Is work for many people merely "hated toil"—they are really not "in" their work; they do not enjoy their work? Why or why not? What makes the difference? What kinds of work, or work in what kinds of situations, seem to you to be fulfilling and satisfying?

3. Do you think there are aspects of our economic system that "pander" to the worst in man? If so, what are they? Could they and should they be eliminated?

4. How would you relate what Marx says about money to the place money actually has in our society, and to what the New Testament has to say about money and wealth? Read, for example: Matt. 6:24; 19:22; Luke 12:33–34; I Tim. 6:10; James 5:1–6; I John 3:17.

5. Is there anything wrong with a society that can only exist through increasing consumption, so that some goods are produced intentionally to have a dated obsolescence?

6. In principle is there anything in the Christian faith that stands against violent revolution as a means to what are believed to be good ends? What about the American Revolution? What are just ends?

Suggestions for further reading: A handy collection of Marx's and Marxist writings is to be found in *Basic Writings on Politics and Philosophy,* edited by Feuer (Anchor Books). John

Bennett's *Christianity and Communism Today* (Association Press paperback) and *The God That Failed,* edited by Richard Crossman (Harper paperback) may also prove interesting.

CHAPTER 5

We can quickly summarize some of the basic issues in Freud. These have to do with the relative importance of the unconscious, sexuality, and what happens in childhood, for the understanding of human existence. Is Freud right about the source of conflict in human life? Are aggression and hostility built into the human organism even apart from the particular circumstances of a given individual's social experience in childhood or after?

One of the most serious questions at stake in Freud's thought has to do with the nature and existence of human freedom. Freud clearly believed that all human behavior is causally determined from behind. Freedom seems to be simply the insight one can have into the determinations that play upon one. Of course this raises the question of responsibility. Are people really responsible for what they do, and if so, what do we then mean by responsibility? Are people who are neurotic or psychotic "sick," in the sense that they are what they are because of conditions over which they have had no control? Are they, on the other hand, in some sense responsible for what they are and have become? The implications of one's position on this issue are interesting for the treatment of crime, and for the activities of the courts in determining guilt.

1. How much control do you think an individual really has over what he does?

2. Do some people have more and some less? If so, what do you think makes the difference?

3. Do you think some people, or perhaps all people, are driven by forces of which they are unaware?

4. Does Freud's view that we forget *for a reason* seem probable to you? Do you suppose that the reason we have forgotten

most of our childhood experiences has something to do with the anxiety they would stir up in us, or might there be other factors involved?

5. Do you think sexuality and its power have been underestimated by most people? How has it been dealt with by Christianity and by the churches? Do you think this has been a realistic response?

6. If the child and what happens to him is as important as Freud thinks, for what the man becomes, then what inference do you draw about the nature of man?

7. What do you think Freud would say about the *Playboy* philosophy?

Suggestions for further reading: A good place to begin the study of Freud is in his *A General Introduction to Psychoanalysis* (available in various paperback editions). His interpretation of religion, *The Future of an Illusion*, is interesting. Freud's views have been criticized by many from within the psychological perspective. Jung and Adler were early critics. Later the so-called Neo-Freudians, Horney, Sullivan, Fromm, who rooted man's difficulties more in social conditions than in some kind of innate conflict, offered a depth psychology, building upon Freud, yet critical of him. These authors are worth study.

Chapter 6

There are many significant issues that might be lifted out of the discussion of Kierkegaard. The following questions may point to some of them:

1. Do you think that Kierkegaard's attempt to sort out the variety of basic orientations to life is worthwhile? Obviously people live very different lives—every family, for example, has a pattern of life somewhat different from that of every other family, but underneath such differences do you recognize what Kierkegaard saw as fundamentally different loyalties and styles of life?

2. What about Kierkegaard's own classification? Looking at yourself or at the people you know best, can you recognize his basic "stages on life's way"?

3. What do you think about his scheme of arranging these "stages" or styles of life in a hierarchy, or along a continuum, taking the position that some of them are nearer and some farther from truly personal existence or from the Christian life?

4. Kierkegaard makes much of anxiety in human life. Why do you think people get anxious? Look first at the particular situations in which they become anxious and then try to see if there is some underlying root of all the examples you consider.

5. Do you think Kierkegaard's view of the "crowd" is basically valid? What happens to the individual in the group or in a mass? Does this always happen? Why or why not?

6. In a group that had heard about Kierkegaard's views that the Christian life involved voluntary suffering and a willingness to suffer for the truth, some responded by saying: "You can't sell that to people, in the churches or out!" What do you think? As you read the New Testament is this a characteristic mark of the Christian life? If it is, where do you find "real Christianity" today?

7. Where in Kierkegaard's analysis would the *Playboy* philosophy fit?

Suggestions for further reading: The best place to begin in reading Kierkegaard is his little work *Purity of Heart* (Harper Torchbook). The heart of his Christian teaching is in *Training in Christianity* (Princeton University Press, 1947). A more detailed analysis of his view of life may be found in *The Prayers of Kierkegaard,* by Perry LeFevre (The University of Chicago Press, Phoenix paperback).

CHAPTER 7

Several of the important issues arising in Buber's thought can be seen in relation to some of the points considered earlier. Vis-à-vis Kierkegaard, for example, what is the relative importance of the interpersonal, the relational, the social, as over against the separated individual—the man alone before God? Which plays the larger part in making the individual what he is and in helping him become what he is meant to be? Where does man meet God—as a "single one" (which is the term Kierkegaard gave to man alone before God) or "in the in-between" (which is the term Buber uses again and again to refer to the relational and the interpersonal)? Does Buber in his view of man adequately separate the positive social relationships from those negative ones Kierkegaard points to when he writes about the crowd?

In relation to Marx one needs to assess the relative merits of Buber's views. Like Marx, Buber wants socialism. He advocates a kind of democratic socialism in which there is only enough centralization of power to do the job and in which there is the decentralized pluralistic nurturing of the various segments of life within society. He wants a society that gives itself quite consciously to developing the fully human life for all its members, and this he thinks can happen only if cooperatives of all sorts form the basis of life within the social organism. Both Marxists and the defenders of capitalism would say he is unrealistic. What do you think?

1. Can you recognize in your own experience examples of Buber's distinction between I-Thou and I-It? Examples?

2. Does Buber's distinction between *seeming* and *being*, *monologue* and *dialogue*, make sense to you?

3. Do you think "events speak to man" in the sense in which Buber means this phrase?

4. What would Freud say to Buber and Buber to Freud?

5. What is your reaction to Buber's view that God is to be found through the relationships between persons and in hallowing the everyday?

6. Buber was sometimes said to be "more of a Christian than many Christians." What do you think would be meant by such a statement? What do you think Buber might say about Jesus?

Suggestions for further reading: One of the best places to get at the heart of Buber's thought is in his essays on education in his book *Between Man and Man* (Beacon Press paperback). Everyone should read his classic work *I and Thou* (Scribner paperback).

CHAPTER 8

1. Do you believe that Niebuhr is correct: that what is wrong with man is that he is self-centered, and the taint of self-interest is on everything he does? Do all men think too highly of themselves?

2. Carl Rogers, the well-known psychotherapist, reviewing Niebuhr's work *The Self and the Dramas of History* declared that most of the people he sees as patients have something quite different wrong with them. They think *too little* of themselves. They have given up or lost all their self-esteem. They may even hate themselves. Have you known such people? Do you think this view should be used to supplement Niebuhr's? If so, is there still a more basic notion of what is wrong with man than that of pride? What might it be?

3. If pride and the taint of self-interest characterize all or most human action, do you think there are important differences of degree in this? Are there differences in the relative destructiveness in the forms that pride and self-interest take? Give some illustrations.

4. Niebuhr seems to assume that man is responsible for his self-centeredness and pride. In the light of Freud's understanding of the power of the unconscious and the importance of childhood experience, can this be true? What do you think Niebuhr would say to Freud's point other than to deny it?

5. There has been a good deal of criticism of Niebuhr's understanding of the meaning of love. For him the highest form of love is selfless love, a love in which there is no concern for self. He thinks man is not really capable of such love.

Do you agree that man can never love in this way? What do you make of the Biblical injunction to love your neighbor *as yourself,* in the light of Niebuhr's understanding of the sinfulness of every kind of self-concern.

6. What would Niebuhr's views of the social implications of the Christian faith, especially with respect to his understanding of the meaning of justice, imply for dealing with the racial question in the United States?

Suggestions for further reading: Niebuhr's story of his days as a parish minister in Detroit, *Leaves from the Notebook of a Tamed Cynic* (Meridian paperback), is a good beginning. *An Interpretation of Christian Ethics* (Meridian paperback) and his two-volume *The Nature and Destiny of Man* (Scribner paperback) are for those who want to penetrate Niebuhr's most provocative thought.

CHAPTER 9

The author's personal views have obviously been expressed in a limited fashion. Central attention has been given to the individual and to the interpersonal dimensions of human life. Matters of major concern to some of the thinkers previously discussed—evolution, the economic organization of production, and the social order—have been largely ignored. Do you believe that the author's views could be effectively related to these larger problems? Why or why not? What form might they take?

The author writes about Christ in relation to man's finding a way to move in the direction of becoming a center of freedom and love. What do you think he might hold to be the relation of the figure of Jesus Christ to his definition of the goal for human life? to the diagnosis of what is wrong with man?

1. What do you believe are the chief impediments to man's
   a. becoming
   b. a center
   c. of freedom
   d. and of love?
2. What helps man to move in this direction?

3. Do you think that much of life does have a "cruciform" character? If so, in what sense is that true?

4. How is trust actually developed between persons? between man and God?

Notes

CHAPTER 1. PERSPECTIVES ON MAN IN POPULAR CULTURE

1. Cf. Herschel Baker, *The Image of Man* (Harper Torchbook, 1961), and S. Radhakrishnan and P. T. Raju, eds., *The Concept of Man* (Johnsen Publishing Co., 1960).

2. From T. S. Eliot, *Selected Prose,* ed. by John Hayward (Penguin Book, 1953), p. 39.

3. From *60 Years of Best Sellers, 1895–1955,* by Alice Payne Hackett (R. R. Bowker Company, 1956), p. 10.

4. From "Mickey Spillane and His Bloody Hammer," by Christopher La Farge in *Mass Culture: The Popular Arts in America,* ed. by Bernard Rosenberg and David M. White (The Free Press of Glencoe, 1957), p. 177.

5. Cf. "A Cosmic View of the Private Eye," by John Paterson in *The Saturday Evening Post,* August 22, 1953. Compare also "Theology and Detective Fiction," by Robert D. Paul, in *Student World,* Vol. 55, No. 2, 1962.

6. From "Simenon and Spillane: The Metaphysics of Murder for the Millions," by Charles J. Rolo, in Rosenberg and White, eds., *op. cit.,* p. 174.

7. Cf. *Playboy,* Vol. II, No. 12 (December, 1964), p. 94.

8. *Commentary,* August, 1962, p. 113.

9. *The Chicago Theological Seminary Register,* November, 1959, p. 34.

10. *Ibid.,* p. 35.

11. From *The Feminine Mystique,* by Betty Friedan (W. W. Norton & Co., Inc., 1963), p. 36.

12. From "The Art of Personal Journalism," by Robert H.

Abel in *The Funnies,* ed. by David M. White and Robert H. Abel (The Free Press of Glencoe, 1963), p. 115.

13. From "The Opinions of Little Orphan Annie and Her Friends," by Lyle W. Sherman in Rosenberg and White, eds., *op. cit.,* p. 215.

14. Quoted by Robert L. Short in *The Gospel According to Peanuts* (John Knox Press, 1964).

CHAPTER 2. JULIAN HUXLEY—MAN IN EVOLUTION—
A HUMANIST VIEW

1. From *New Bottles for New Wine,* by Julian Huxley (Harper & Brothers, 1957), p. 43. This work has also been published in paperback under the title *Knowledge, Morality and Destiny* (Mentor Book, 1960) with a different pagination.

2. *Ibid.,* p. 45.

3. *Ibid.,* pp. 27–28.

4. *Ibid.,* p. 39.

5. *Ibid.,* p. 50.

6. From "The Evolutionary Vision," by Julian Huxley, in *Evolution After Darwin,* Vol. III, *Issues in Evolution: The University of Chicago Centennial Discussions,* ed. by Sol Tax and Charles Callender (The University of Chicago Press, 1960), p. 251.

7. *New Bottles for New Wine,* p. 49.

8. *Ibid.,* p. 103.

9. *Ibid.,* p. 13.

10. *Ibid.,* p. 70.

11. *Ibid.,* p. 112.

12. *Ibid.,* p. 238.

13. *Ibid.,* p. 59.

14. From *The Humanist Frame,* ed. by Julian Huxley (London: George Allen & Unwin, Ltd., 1962), p. 33.

15. *Ibid.,* p. 24.

16. *Ibid.*

17. *Ibid.,* p. 25.

18. *New Bottles for New Wine,* p. 276.

19. *Ibid.*, p. 277.

20. *Ibid.*, p. 116.

21. *Ibid.*

22. *Ibid.*, p. 296.

23. *Ibid.*

24. *Ibid.*, p. 127.

25. From *The Human Crisis,* by Julian Huxley (University of Washington Press, 1963), p. 23.

26. *New Bottles for New Wine,* p. 237.

CHAPTER 3. TEILHARD DE CHARDIN—MAN IN EVOLUTION— A CHRISTIAN VIEW

1. Quoted in *Pierre Teilhard de Chardin,* by C. Tresmontant (Helicon Press, 1959), p. 14.

2. From *The Phenomenon of Man,* by Pierre Teilhard de Chardin (Harper Torchbook, 1961), p. 29.

3. From *The Future of Man,* by Pierre Teilhard de Chardin (Harper & Row, Publishers, Inc., 1964), p. 84.

4. *Ibid.*, p. 12.

5. *Ibid.*, p. 105.

6. *Ibid.*, p. 111.

7. *Ibid.*, p. 65.

8. *Ibid.*, p. 69.

9. *Ibid.*, p. 131.

10. *Ibid.*, p. 132.

11. *Ibid.*

12. *Ibid.*, p. 133.

13. *Ibid.*, p. 42.

14. *Ibid.*, p. 44.

15. *Ibid.*, pp. 46–47.

16. From *The Phenomenon of Man,* p. 258.

17. *Ibid.*, p. 262.

18. *Ibid.*, p. 263.

19. *Ibid.*, p. 265.

20. *Ibid.*, p. 264.

21. *Ibid.*, p. 267.

22. *Ibid.*, p. 269.
23. *Ibid.*, p. 270.
24. *Ibid.*, p. 291.
25. *Ibid.*, pp. 291–292.
26. *Ibid.*, p. 293.
27. *Ibid.*, pp. 293–294.
28. *Ibid.*, p. 294.
29. *Ibid.*, p. 296.
30. *Ibid.*, pp. 296–297.
31. Quoted by the editor in *The Divine Milieu,* by Pierre Teilhard de Chardin (Harper & Brothers, 1960), p. 14.
32. *Ibid.*
33. *Ibid.*, p. 15.
34. *Ibid.*, p. 27.
35. *Ibid.*, p. 30.
36. *Ibid.*, p. 31.
37. *Ibid.*, p. 33.
38. *Ibid.*, p. 62.
39. *Ibid.*, p. 79.
40. *Ibid.*, p. 85.
41. *Ibid.*, p. 89.
42. *Ibid.*, p. 90.
43. *Ibid.*, p. 100.
44. *Ibid.*, p. 101.
45. *Ibid.*, p. 103.
46. *Ibid.*, p. 124.
47. *Ibid.*, p. 139.
48. *Ibid.*, p. 137.

CHAPTER 4. KARL MARX—ECONOMIC MAN

1. Quoted in *Human Nature, the Marxian View,* by Vernon Venable (Alfred A. Knopf, Inc., 1945), pp. 124–125.
2. *Ibid.*, p. 30.
3. From *The German Ideology,* by Karl Marx and F. Engels (International Publishers Co., Inc., 1939), p. 7. I am indebted

to Mr. Gabriel Fackre for calling attention to this reference and for several later references to Marx's *Capital*.

4. From *The Economic and Philosophical Manuscripts of Karl Marx* (hereinafter cited as *Economic and Philosophical Manuscripts*), tr. by T. B. Bottomore in *Marx's Concept of Man*, by E. Fromm (Frederick Ungar Publishing Company, 1961), p. 95.

5. The value contained in a certain commodity is equal to the labor time required for its production. Marx writes about surplus value in the third volume of *Capital*.

6. From *Economic and Philosophical Manuscripts*, pp. 95–96.

7. From *Capital*, by Karl Marx (Foreign Languages Publishing House, 1961), Vol. I, p. 645.

8. From *Economic and Philosophical Manuscripts*, pp. 98–99.

9. From *Capital*, I, pp. 264–265.

10. *Ibid.*, I, pp. 244, 247–248.

11. *Ibid.*, III, p. 88.

12. *Economic and Philosophical Manuscripts*, pp. 140–142.

13. From *A World Without Jews*, by Karl Marx (Philosophical Library, Inc., 1959), p. 40.

14. *Economic and Philosophical Manuscripts*, p. 164.

15. *Ibid.*, p. 168.

16. *Capital*, I, p. 645.

17. *Economic and Philosophical Manuscripts*, p. 127.

18. *Ibid.*, p. 132.

19. *Ibid.*, p. 138.

20. *Capital*, III, p. 800.

21. From *A Handbook of Marxism*, ed. by E. Burns (Random House, Inc., 1935), p. 47.

22. *Ibid.*, p. 985.

CHAPTER 5. SIGMUND FREUD—PSYCHOLOGICAL MAN

1. From *Autobiography*, by Sigmund Freud (W. W. Norton & Company, Inc., 1935), p. 25.

2. From *Studies in Hysteria,* by Joseph Breuer and Sigmund Freud (Beacon Press, 1958), p. 23.

3. *Ibid.*

4. From *Civilization and Its Discontents,* by Sigmund Freud (Doubleday Anchor Book, 1958), pp. 60–61.

5. *Ibid.,* p. 16.

6. *Ibid.*

7. *Ibid.,* p. 43.

8. *Ibid.,* p. 72.

9. *Ibid.,* p. 77.

10. *Ibid.,* p. 90.

11. *Ibid.,* p. 92.

12. This and the following paragraph are drawn from the author's review of Philip Rieff's excellent work, *Freud, the Mind of a Moralist* (The Viking Press, Inc., 1959), which appeared in *The Christian Scholar,* Vol. XLIII, No. 4 (Winter, 1960).

13. See Sigmund Freud, "Analysis Terminable and Interminable" in *Collected Papers* (London: Hogarth Press, Ltd., 1950), Vol. V.

14. From *Civilization and Its Discontents,* p. 103.

15. *Ibid.,* p. 104.

16. *Ibid.,* p. 105.

CHAPTER 6. SØREN KIERKEGAARD—EXISTENTIAL MAN

1. From *The Point of View,* by Søren Kierkegaard (Harper Torchbook, 1962), p. 112.

2. From *The Journals of Søren Kierkegaard,* a selection edited and translated by Alexander Dru (Oxford University Press, 1938), entry 149, p. 49.

3. *Ibid.,* entry 962, p. 331.

4. *Ibid.,* entry 150, p. 50.

CHAPTER 7. MARTIN BUBER—MAN IN DIALOGUE

1. From "The William Alanson White Memorial Lectures, Fourth Series," by Martin Buber in *Psychiatry,* Vol. XX, No. 2 (May, 1957), p. 111.

2. From *The Way of Man,* by Martin Buber (Wilcox & Follett Company, 1951), p. 25.

3. From *Good and Evil,* by Martin Buber (Charles Scribner's Sons, 1953), p. 127.

4. From *At the Turning,* by Martin Buber (Farrar, Straus & Young, Inc., 1952), p. 49.

5. From *I and Thou* (2d ed.), by Martin Buber (Charles Scribner's Sons, 1958), p. 75.

6. *Ibid.,* p. 76.

7. *Ibid.,* p. 79.

8. From *Eclipse of God,* by Martin Buber (Harper Torchbook, 1957), p. 36.

9. From *At the Turning,* p. 37.

10. From *Eclipse of God,* p. 166.

11. From *Paths in Utopia,* by Martin Buber (Beacon Press, Inc., 1958), p. 129.

12. *Ibid.,* pp. 131–132.

13. From *Between Man and Man,* by Martin Buber (London: Kegan Paul, Trench, Trubner & Co., 1947), pp. 31–32.

14. From *Paths in Utopia,* p. 130.

15. *Ibid.,* p. 137.

16. *Ibid.,* p. 128.

17. *Ibid.,* p. 137.

18. *Ibid.,* p. 133.

19. From *Pointing the Way,* tr. by Maurice Friedman (Harper & Brothers, 1957), p. 114.

CHAPTER 8. REINHOLD NIEBUHR—MAN AS SINNER

1. From *Faith and History,* by Reinhold Niebuhr (Charles Scribner's Sons, 1949), p. 118.

2. From *The Nature and Destiny of Man,* Vol. I, by Reinhold Niebuhr (Charles Scribner's Sons, 1941), p. 182.

3. *Ibid.,* p. 199.

4. *Ibid.,* p. 200.

5. *Ibid.,* p. 277.

6. From "Ten Years That Shook My World," by Reinhold

Niebuhr, in *The Christian Century*, Vol. 56 (April 26, 1939), pp. 542–546.

7. From *The Nature and Destiny of Man*, Vol. II, by Reinhold Niebuhr (Charles Scribner's Sons, 1943), p. 98.

8. *Ibid.*, pp. 107 ff.

9. *Ibid.*, p. 121.

10. *Ibid.*, p. 123.

11. *Ibid.*, p. 125.

12. *Ibid.*, p. 85.

13. From *Christian Faith and Social Action*, ed. by John Hutchison (Charles Scribner's Sons, 1953), p. 238.

14. *Ibid.*, p. 241.

15. From *An Interpretation of Christian Ethics*, by Reinhold Niebuhr (Living Age Book, 1956), p. 136.

16. From *The Nature and Destiny of Man*, Vol. II, p. 254.

17. From *An Interpretation of Christian Ethics*, p. 134.

18. See "Biblical Faith and Socialism: A Critical Appraisal," by Reinhold Niebuhr in *Religion and Culture*, ed. by W. Leibrecht (Harper & Brothers, 1959).

19. From "Human Creativity and Self-Concern in Freud's Thought," by Reinhold Niebuhr in *Freud and the 20th Century*, ed. by B. Nelson (Meridian Book, 1957), p. 269.

CHAPTER 9. A PERSONAL VIEWPOINT

1. Some of the ideas developed in this chapter were stated in a more limited way in *Pastoral Psychology*, December, 1960.

2. From *Surprised by Joy*, by C. S. Lewis (London: Geoffrey Bles, Ltd., 1955), quoted in *The Faith of an Artist*, ed. by John Wilson (London: George Allen & Unwin, 1962), p. 108.

3. From "Handle with Care," by F. Scott Fitzgerald, in *Esquire* magazine, March, 1936, collected in *The Crack-Up*, ed. by Edmund Wilson (New Directions, 1945), pp. 78–79.

4. From *Hold Me!* by Jules Feiffer (Signet Book, New American Library, 1964), pp. 92–95.

5. From *Afternoon of a Pawnbroker and Other Poems*, by Kenneth Fearing (Harcourt, Brace and World, Inc., 1943), pp. 19–21.

6. Cf. *Being and Nothingness,* by Jean-Paul Sartre (Philosophical Library, Inc., 1956), Ch. 2.

7. From *Escape from Loneliness,* by Paul Tournier (The Westminster Press, 1962), p. 13.

8. From *Peanuts,* by Charles Schulz (United Feature Syndicate, Inc., 1963).

9. See "The Anatomy of Loneliness," by Thomas Wolfe, *American Mercury,* Vol. LIII, No. 214 (October, 1941), p. 467.

10. Cf. *Training in Christianity,* tr. by Walter Lowrie (Princeton University Press, 1944).

11. From *The Word Incarnate,* by Norman Pittenger (Harper & Brothers, 1959), p. 180.

12. From *The Interpretation of the Fourth Gospel,* by C. H. Dodd (London: Cambridge University Press, 1953), p. 285.

13. From *Between Man and Man,* by Martin Buber (London: Kegan Paul, Trench, Trubner & Co., 1947), p. 98.

CHAPTER 10. THE NATURE AND DESTINY OF MAN—
UNANSWERED QUESTIONS

1. From *Reinhold Niebuhr: A Prophetic Voice in Our Time,* ed. by H. R. Landon (The Seabury Press, Inc., 1962), pp. 34, 120.

2. From *Knowledge, Morality and Destiny,* by Julian Huxley (Mentor Book, 1960), pp. 210–211.